MOHANDAS K. GANDHI

A BIOGRAPHY

MOHANDAS K. GANDHI

A BIOGRAPHY

PATRICIA CRONIN MARCELLO

JAICO PUBLISHING HOUSE

Ahmedabad Bangalore Chennai
Delhi Hyderabad Kolkata Mumbai

Published by Jaico Publishing House
A-2 Jash Chambers, 7-A Sir Phirozshah Mehta Road
Fort, Mumbai - 400 001
jaicopub@jaicobooks.com
www.jaicobooks.com

Originally published in hard cover by Greenwood Press,
an imprint of ABC-CLIO, LLC
Santa Barbara, CA

Published in arrangement with
ABC-CLIO, LLC, Santa Barbara, CA

MOHANDAS K. GANDHI
ISBN 978-81-8495-359-6

First Jaico Impression: 2012
Second Jaico Impression: 2014

Printed by
Trinity Academy For Corporate Training Limited, Mumbai

To my sister, Barbara, whom I will always love and admire, and to Milt, Rick, Bob, Ron, Dianne, and Donna, their wives and husbands, and all their children—the best family in the world.

CONTENTS

Introduction ix

Timeline of Events in the Life of Mohandas K. Gandhi xi

Chapter 1 Tradition and Duty 1

Chapter 2 Becoming an English Gentleman 15

Chapter 3 India from a Different Point of View 29

Chapter 4 Awakening a Diminutive Giant 43

Chapter 5 A Catalyst for Change 57

Chapter 6 Rebounding to the Transvaal 71

Chapter 7 Trust and Disappointment 87

Chapter 8 An End to Satyagraha in South Africa 99

Chapter 9 First Steps to Freedom 115

Chapter 10 A Free India and an Unholy Death 137

Glossary 159

Selected Bibliography 161

Index 163

INTRODUCTION

Many call Mohandas K. Gandhi the father of modern India because he was the primary leader in the Indian quest to achieve independence from England, a country that had ruled India for almost 100 years. He was a spiritual person, often perceived as mystical. Throngs came from afar to see him, just for a spiritual blessing *(deshan)* derived merely from being in his presence. His people called him *Mahatma*, an Indian word meaning "great soul," and one could say he was revered more than respected. His power arose from his subtlety and his doctrine of nonviolence, though his ideals were not easily upheld by the masses. Gandhi was in the right place in India's heart when scholar Bal Gangadhar Tilak, an early proponent of Indian Home Rule, died in 1920. People like Tilak and Annie Besant began the push for Home Rule while Gandhi was strengthening his political legs in South Africa, but Gandhi was the one who led India to independence in 1947.

The British underestimated him. Indian politicians used him to inspire the people but, during his later years, they set him aside as a doddering old man when younger men disagreed with his ways. Still, the movement came to realize that only Gandhi could control the hearts and minds of the people of India.

In researching this work, many sources were consulted, most of which came directly from Gandhi himself, via his autobiography, his recounting of the South African struggle for Indian equality in *Satyagraha in South Africa*, and his myriad volumes of collected works, all found online. Other sources include government documents, other works by Gandhi and other biographers, as well as magazines, newspapers, and the diaries of his secretary, Mahadev H. Desai. Other reliable Internet sources are listed in the bibliography.

TIMELINE OF EVENTS IN THE LIFE OF MOHANDAS K. GANDHI

October 2, 1869	Born in Porbandar, Gujarat, India
1883	Married Kasturba Kapadia of Porbandar
September 4, 1888	Left India for London to study law
June 10, 1891	Called to the British Bar and enrolled in the High Court
June 12, 1891	Returned to India
May 24, 1892	Went to Bombay to practice law
April 1893	Set sail for South Africa to settle case for Dada Abdullah and Company
August 22, 1894	Founded the Natal Indian Congress
August 14, 1896	Published *Green Pamphlet* at Rajkot
October 17, 1899	Joined ambulance corps during Boer War in South Africa
October 1, 1904	Assumed management of *The Indian Opinion* newspaper
November–December 1904	Founded the Phoenix Settlement to run newspaper and house workers and family.
September 1906	Began policy of nonviolent resistance *(Satyagraha)* to protest Indian registration requirements
November 13–22, 1906	Wrote *Hind Swaraj* aboard the *SS Kildonan Castle*, bound for South Africa, after a trip to London to promote awareness of South African situation

May 30, 1910	Founded Tolstoy Farm near Johannesburg, South Africa
May 14, 1913	Indian marriages invalidated by South African court
October 17, 1913	Sent women of Phoenix compound into Natal to incite Indian miners to strike against unfair treatment
November 3, 1913	Announced march into Transvaal with army of protestors from Natal
November 11, 1913	Sentenced to nine months in prison at hard labor for taking indentured laborers across the Natal border
December 18, 1914	Released from prison unconditionally
January 13–16, 1914	Met with General Smuts and came to agreement. *Satyagraha* is suspended.
July 18, 1914	Sailed for England
August 4, 1914	England declared war on Germany and Gandhi volunteered to organize another ambulance corps.
December 19, 1914	In poor health, returned to India
May 20, 1915	Founded *Satyagraha Sabha*, also known as *Sabarmati Ashram*
April 1917	Traveled to Champaran to assess complaints of mistreatment by Indian indigo workers
January–March 1918	Initiated *Satyagraha* in Kheda because of tax dispute with British Indian government
April 27, 1918	Attended Viceroy's war conference
February 24, 1919	Signed *Satyagraha* Pledge in order to have harsh restrictions of Rowlatt Act repealed
April 6, 1919	Began India-wide *Satyagraha*
April 13, 1919	Jallianwalla Bagh massacre of Indian festival participants by British troops
November 24, 1919	Presided over Khilafat Conference in Delhi
August 1, 1920	Surrendered medals won in Zulu and Boer Wars to the Viceroy
December 1920	Indian National Congress at Calcutta approved program of noncooperation to attain *Swaraj* (freedom)
August 1921	Lit huge bonfire of European clothing in Bombay, setting off boycott of all foreign cloth

February 1922	Notified Viceroy of intent to launch *Satyagraha* campaign in Bardoli
February 4, 1922	Chauri Chaura riot at police station
March 10, 1922	Arrested for sedition and sentenced to six years in jail
January 12, 1924	Surgery performed for appendicitis
February 5, 1924	Released from jail because of poor health
September 24, 1925	Founded All-India Spinners' Association
November 1925	Began writing autobiography
January 26, 1930	*Purna Swaraj* Day established to celebrate the Indian commitment to achieve complete independence
March 2, 1930	Gave Viceroy notice of intent to break laws that taxed salt
May 5, 1930	Arrest for sedition
February 18, 1931	Began series of talks regarding Indian independence with Viceroy Irwin, resulting in pact
September 15, 1931	Presented India's demand for complete independence at Federal Structure Committee meeting (Round Table Conference)
February 23, 1933	First issue of *The Harijan* newspaper published
July 30, 1933	Warned government of revival of civil disobedience
August 1, 1933	Arrested and imprisoned without trial for threatening general boycott of foreign cloth and liquor
August 16, 1933	Fasted because of lack of facility to publish *The Harijan* while in prison
September 17, 1934	Announced retirement from politics
October 26, 1934	Founded the All-India Village Industries Association
March 27, 1942	Met Sir Stafford Cripps in New Delhi
February 22, 1944	Death of Kasturba during incarceration
May 1, 1947	Congress Working Committee accepted partition policy and formation of Pakistan
July 1947	Passage of Independence of India Bill
September 2, 1947	Retreat house where staying mobbed
January 20, 1948	Hand grenade exploded at prayer meeting
January 30, 1948	Assassinated by a Hindu who was harboring resentment over the split of India and the creation of Pakistan

Chapter 1

TRADITION AND DUTY

On October 2, 1869, Mohandas Karamchand Gandhi was born in India into a changing world. In the United States, feminist and suffragette Elizabeth Cady Stanton had become the first woman to testify before Congress; Civil War hero and general, Ulysses S. Grant, had assumed the presidency; and the last spike in the transcontinental railway was driven at Promontory, Utah, permitting overland transportation from the East Coast to the West Coast. In other places around the world, the Hudson Bay Company ceded sovereignty over its vast territorial holdings to Canada, the Suez Canal was opened, and Pope Pius IX presided over the first Vatican Council in Rome. The latter part of the nineteenth century was tumultuous and expansive, and in the dark recesses of India, where poverty, hunger, and hard labor held sway, people had no idea that an old soul, a *mahatma*, would soon emerge.

Gandhi was known as Moniya or Mohan as a child and was the youngest of four children. His three older siblings were brother Laxmidas, born 1863; brother Karsandas, born 1866; and sister, Raliatben, born 1862. He also had two older stepsisters; Gandhi's father, Karamchand (Kaba), was married four times, three times widowed.

Kaba was the son of Uttamchand (Ota) Gandhi, who had been a prime minister in Porbandar, India, situated on the Kathiawar peninsula in the northwestern coastal province of Gujarat. Arabs, Dutch, Portuguese, Persian, and British merchants all left their mark on the area, as Porbandar was a major port on the Arabian Sea. In the 1870 census, the town showed a population of 72,000 people.[1] Porbandar was known for its limestone, which was rather clayish in consistency. During rainstorms, the limestone outside any structure would harden to resemble marble, making for a firm construction; therefore, mortar was never used in a Porbandar limestone building. The luminosity of the material gave the city a superior whiteness, and so it was nicknamed the White City. Its streets were narrow and crowded, as were its small homes that held extended families.

Though the name *Gandhi* translates into English as grocer. Mohandas, his father, and uncles followed Ota's political line. Kaba was the fifth of six brothers, and both he and his youngest brother were prime ministers in the city of Porbandar, in succession. In this position, each had influence over different clans in the area and often settled disputes that arose among the tribesmen. Kaba wore a gold chain to signify his office, and his position afforded the Gandhi family the appearance of comfort and erudition, which set the Gandhi children apart from the other children of the village. Yet, the family was not wealthy, and at the time of Kaba's death, there was very little estate to pass on.

Gandhi's strong religious heritage came from Putliba, his mother. She was a staunch Hindu and was close to Gandhi. His spirituality seems to have grown from her example. She followed strict abstinence of alcohol, tobacco, and meat in any form, as traditions of her religious values, although she showed the children this moral code, rather than preaching it to them. Her children adored her and often watched her fasting and going to the Vaishnava temple daily, where she would worship the Hindu god Vishnu. They thought of her as a saint.

Putliba was merely 15 when she married Kaba, who was in his forties. Such age differences were common in India, and it was standard for widowers to marry again so they would have another housekeeper and mother for their children. As life expectancy in India was under 30 years of age at the time, Kaba was quite advanced in age—yet he was robust. With Putliba, he fathered four more children. Gandhi wrote, "My father was a lover of his clan, truthful, brave and generous, but short-tempered. To a certain extent he might have been given to carnal pleasures.... But he was incorruptible and had earned a name for strict impartiality in his family as well as outside."[2]

Kaba's position also provided Gandhi greater freedom in Porbandar. He knew most of the boys there and was very curious. His devoted nurse, Rambha, had a very hard time keeping up with him, as he was constantly sneaking away to climb trees or to follow ceremonial parades. To the disdain of his elders, the mischievous boy once moved a religious statue from its recess in the family's prayer room so that he could sit in the niche himself.

A NEW LIFE IN AN OLD TOWN

When Gandhi was seven years old, the family moved from Porbandar to Rajkot, an adjacent eastern district in the Gujarati province. Kaba had become a member of the Rajasthanik Court. Though still under control of the British Empire, as it had been since 1858 when Queen Victoria declared the country a British Crown Colony, Gujarat was more like a protectorate than a true colonial state. There and elsewhere in India, princes governed their own districts, though they were puppets of the British government. Most princes were authoritarian and squelched any anti-Anglo sentiments among their subjects as soon as they arose to stay in the good graces of the British Raj (rule).

Gandhi's father held the position of chief minister (*diwan*) and was subject to transfer at any time among the friendly neighboring districts of Rajkot or Wankaner, as the whim moved the princes to shuffle their administrators. As had been true for the Gandhis, most appointments for minor political positions were based on family ties or obligations, rather than ability. Kaba had inherited his position from his father, and when he moved from Porbandar, his brother moved in to take his place there. Most often, these appointed offices were held by Hindus, as they made up the majority of the population, and most Hindu appointees were from the appropriate caste, though the Gandhis were neither of the proper nor the superior caste.

This social hierarchy, or caste system (which still exists in modern India), is based in Hindu mythology, which holds that all men were originally created Brahmins, considered the highest caste, and they hold the traditional occupations of priests or teachers. Hindus believe that lower castes were created via men's behaviors. The Kshatriyas, the second caste, are considered passionate, making them warriors and rulers. The Gandhis belonged to the third-ranked caste, the Vaishnavas, who are traditionally traders, cattlemen, farmers, and artisans, and are known as the arms and legs of Indian society because they do most of the work. The fourth-ranked caste, the Sudras, are seen as having fallen away from purity in a former life, which made them vulnerable to the element of darkness, and by consequence are traditionally charged with the performance of menial labor. These four groups are the basic Varnas, which do not indicate class or status, but rather skin color. Among these Varnas are thousands of subcastes and subcultures, called Jats or Jatis, and even those in the same Varna looked down on those in a lower Jat. This system dictates not only a person's occupation but also their dietary regimen and sets guidelines by which castes may interact with one another.

The Sudras are not considered the lowest class of people in India, however. Those people are said to be without caste and are today called the Dalits. In earlier times, they were known as the Untouchables. Dalits are treated as no more than slaves and are reduced to cleaning human feces and dead animals from the streets with their hands. They could not use the same wells as members of higher castes, and their children were forced to sit in the back of classrooms. They lived in extreme poverty and had no prospects for the future. Hindus who followed the caste system had no compassion for these people and believed that the Untouchables were repaying a debt of karma from a previous life. Karma signifies cause and effect and is closely tied with reincarnation, the constant birth, death, and rebirth of one's soul. Negative behaviors in life are still thought to cause negative effects in the life to follow.

Purity and pollution are the two ends of the spectrum that drive the caste system. Higher castes were considered untainted, but the purity also extends to ritual cleanliness. Daily baths, clean clothing of approved materials, and even the food a person ate were important to maintaining a healthy spirit, although this cleansing may have been negated by physical contact with a person of a lower caste. Bodily wastes from another person were considered to produce death or violence and were avoided by all Varnas, as were improper diets. Brahmins are still often vegetarians and avoid eating meat, which is considered a product of violence and death, whereas Kshatriyas eat meat for strength and courage, which is a practice appropriate to their position in life. Today, many educated and urban Indians do not follow the caste practices; however, most of those still living in rural areas are bound by its rules.

The Gandhi family was of the Modh Bania subcaste of Vaishnavas—the merchants—and Gandhi believed that his ancestors had been grocers until his grandfather was appointed an administrator, which made the family an exception to the caste rule. Although Gandhi's father had no formal education, he was above bribery and intrigue in his position and well respected for his ability to manage people. He had been in Porbandar 20 years when he was moved to the eastern district.

ELEMENTARY LESSONS

When the family arrived at Rajkot, Gandhi was put directly into school to finish his primary education, but he was only a mediocre student and painfully shy. At 12 years of age, he was promoted to the high school. Still unable to relate to his classmates, he would appear at the first bell and rush home at the end of the day. Gandhi's most important memory of his earliest years is that he never told a lie; however, he remembered at least one occasion when such honesty had been unrewarding.

Periodically, a school superintendent would come in and test the students to see how the classes were progressing, and every teacher hoped for a favorable report. Gandhi's class was given a spelling test of only five words; one was the word *kettle*, which Gandhi spelled with only one "t." Upon seeing this mistake, his teacher gestured for Gandhi to copy from his neighbor, but Gandhi did not catch on. The entire class spelled every word properly, except for Gandhi, and the teacher chastised him for being so stupid. Through the experience, Gandhi learned to follow orders from an elder, without analyzing them. In that way, he could not be held accountable. Only the person who gave the order was to blame, and in this way, he reconciled departures from the truth, as he would never lie.

One of Gandhi's pastimes outside the classroom was playing the concertina. Around this time, he was also captivated by two plays. The first, *Shravana Pitribhakti Nataka*, was about a Hindu boy's love for his parents. One early passage illustrates this devotion: "My parents are old and blind. I am taking them to pilgrimage all over this noble land of Bharata (India). I carry them on my shoulders in huge baskets attached to the bamboo with the ropes."[3] Gandhi respected and loved both his parents and identified closely with the main character. After reading the play, he was moved to be ever more solicitous to their wants and needs.

The other play, which had a lifelong impact on Gandhi, was titled *Harischandra*. Based in Hindu mythology, the play recounts the trials of King Harischandra, who was tormented by two sages to test his devotion to the truth. No matter the hardships to himself or to his family, Harischandra continued to follow the true path. This complete dedication to the truth, which Gandhi came to equate with God, made an indelible mark on him. As he read the play for the first time, he believed that it was a true story and later wrote, "The thought of it all often made me weep."[4]

Another life-altering change came to Gandhi when he was 13 years old: He was married, a union arranged through proper Hindu rituals. His future wife had been chosen when Gandhi was around 7 years old. Even at such a tender age, she was his third betrothed. The girls involved in the two previously arranged unions died before it was time for marriage.

Kasturba Kapadia of Porbandar, Gandhi's fiancée, had been born around the same time as Gandhi, though no formal records were kept in India at that time. Kasturba was the middle child of the family and had an older and a younger brother. Her father owned the family trading company, which sold cloth, grain, and cotton, and was quite prosperous, although the family lived modestly. In such a small town, it is conceivable that the Gandhi boys and the Kapadia boys, who were all around the same age, played together.

However, Kasturba would not have been involved in any playtime with the boys, as genders were kept separate almost from birth. Girls were married very young, so they had to learn to care for a house and a family. At an age when modern children attend kindergarten, Kasturba was baking bread and washing clothes. Indian logic held that if a woman was to spend her full life in her husband's house, she should accustom herself to such a life from the time she was a small child.

A PRETEEN UNION

Early marriages were the standard in India at that time, and in some parts of the country, child marriages still occur today. Indians reason that this ensures the bride's purity on her wedding day. As the chances for rape or kidnapping by neighboring tribes was high in earlier times, early weddings protected daughters from such fate. Indian fathers married daughters off at a very young age, regardless of the fact that marriage alone would not stop rape or kidnapping. However, it did stop sexual intimacy before marriage and unwanted advances by other men. Even in modern India, men and women are treated separately in many instances, and although rules are no longer quite as strict in India's big cities, husbands and fathers are still supremely protective of women in rural areas, where women's rights are virtually nil.

Choosing a mate near the turn of the century was also a father's right, although the selection must be approved by both parents. The Kapadias were interested in finding a suitable partner for their daughter, and what better choice than a neighbor's son, of whose background there could be no question? The bond was set to be fulfilled later, when both children would be around 13 years of age. Mohan did not even attend the finalization of the betrothal pact; he was only told about it much later. Kasturba had no idea what had transpired but was delighted by the presents she received that day.

Six years after the betrothal, the families began to think about a wedding. Thirteen was actually quite late for Kasturba to become a wife; most Indian marriages took place when girls were around eight years old. It was conceivable that her parents allowed their only daughter to remain unmarried for so long because they were more concerned for her welfare than for the opinion of their neighbors.

The wedding of Mohan and Kasturba would be a colossal affair. Mohan's oldest brother, Laxmidas, was already married; however, his middle brother, Karsandas was not, and since Hindu weddings are such enormous expense, Kaba decided to marry the brothers off at the same time. Moreover, Kaba's nephew, Motilal Gandhi, was also unmarried at seventeen, which was long overdue, so a triple wedding was planned by the Gandhi clan to save on expenses.

Costs for Hindu weddings are still extraordinarily high, largely due to the workings of the caste system. In Gandhi's time, virtually all residents of the town were invited, and because of caste practices, certain expenses became requirements. For instance, they had to hire a high-ranking cook to prepare the food, usually a Brahmin. Since Brahmins can only eat food prepared by other Brahmins, and all lower-caste members can eat food prepared by members of this highest caste, Brahmin cooks were the logical choice. A variety of foods was also required to suit every guest. Yet, these expenses were not decided on by the brides' families, or by the grooms' families. The guest list, the menu, and the entertainment were prescribed by the community council (the Modh Bania caste council in Porbandar, in this case), in accordance with the social status of the brides' parents. Families who wished to uphold their social status complied with the council's wishes, regardless of the expense, and would often go into debt just to satisfy expectations. A triple ceremony was cost-effective, although the arrangement would have been most beneficial to the parents of the brides, because they paid for most of the wedding. A hall had to be hired for the Gandhi wedding and there were decorations, flowers, and extra musicians. Carriages and horses had to be rented, and trousseaus and wedding garments had to be made.

NUPTIAL PREPARATIONS

The Gandhis were to travel to Porbandar for the wedding, which was 125 miles from Rajkot or a five-day journey via oxcart. Just before the trip began, Kaba learned that he had urgent business to attend to before he could leave Rajkot and sent the family ahead without him. He reassured everyone he had been offered the Prince's fastest horses and carriage to carry him to the wedding once the business was complete, and promised not to be late for the service.

After arriving in Porbandar, the wedding participants went through several rituals. The day before the wedding, they were anointed with a fragrant cream called *pithi*, composed of almond, sandalwood, and turmeric. On the day of the big event, the brides were given ceremonial baths with perfumed water, their hair was done, intricate designs were painted on their hands and feet with a paste made from henna leaves, and scarlet *kumkum* marks were made on their foreheads as signs of blessing. They were dressed in beautiful saris, the traditional dress of Indian women.

Bridegrooms were dressed in traditional wedding clothing. Each wore *pijamos*, which are full leggings, or dhotis, which are pantaloon-type trousers, also made from folded lengths of cloth, and a *kafni*, a long shirt that extends to the knees. The grooms may also have worn turbans.

As the preparations were nearing completion, there was great concern, as Kaba had not yet arrived. Meanwhile, Kaba was racing over rough dirt roads in the royal carriage asking if the horses could go no faster, when the wheels of the carriage hit a rock. The transport tumbled over, throwing Kaba to the ground. Although he arrived covered in cuts and bruises, he had completed the journey in three days, rather than the standard five, and made it to the wedding on time. He told the family not to be concerned, that his injuries looked worse than they were, and that he would be fine, as soon as he cleaned up. At the time, he did not realize the seriousness of his wounds and insisted that the wedding go on as planned.

The brides were brought to the wedding hall in one carriage. Inside the building were three canopies, called *mandaps*, where the actual ceremonies would occur. The tent poles were decorated with flowers, and at the bottom of each pole was a pyramid of brass pots.

While the veiled brides awaited their grooms, a wedding procession was taking place on the streets of Porbandar. Each groom was mounted on a mare, which was also decorated in flowers. As the boys traveled to the wedding hall, their mothers and other female relatives accompanied them on foot, singing special wedding songs. Behind them were other relatives, friends, and other townspeople who cared to join in the festivities.

TAKING A WIFE

After Gandhi was inside the tent, he was seated on a low wooden stool facing east; Kasturba was then brought in by her maternal uncle. She was seated on her own stool, facing west. The priest then began to recite the wedding ceremony in Sanskrit. When the prayers were through, Kasturba's father rose from his seat in the tent, holding three blades of grass, while announcing the distinct time and place the marriage was taking place. He then publicly announced his intention of giving his healthy daughter to Gandhi and relinquished all paternal claims on her. He placed the couple's hands together, with a blade of grass separating their palms.

Still seated, but now side by side, the couple waited while the priest recited more prayers. Then, it was time for them to perform the *Saptapadi*—the Seven Steps. They stood side by side and took the first step together as husband and wife, reciting verses they had memorized specially for the occasion. After feeding each other the ceremonial *kansar*, which is a sweet wheat paste, the couple was forever joined.

That night, after the ceremony, Gandhi related how he played the husband and wrote, "Two innocent children all unwittingly hurled themselves into the ocean of life."[5] Although he had been coached by his sister-in-law regarding the wedding night, he also wrote, "But no coaching is really necessary in such matters. The impressions of the former firth are potent enough to make all coaching superfluous."[6]

This passage alludes to the Hindu belief in reincarnation, whereby an individual's soul returns to the earth repeatedly, until it reaches total enlightenment and is released from *samsara*, the cycle of death and rebirth. This liberation is known to the Hindus as *nirvana*, the ultimate goal of existence. Through *samsara*, each soul carries impressions (*samskaras*) into each new life. These *samskaras* regarding sexuality are what Gandhi meant by "impressions of the former firth." No coaching was required for something he had done in a former life.

Yet, if he was a husband in a former life, he had difficulty recalling other *samskaras*. He took to reading pamphlets written for young married people regarding love, thrift, sex, and other topics pertaining to wedded bliss; however, by his own admission, Gandhi ignored the passages he did not like. Jealousy was a major factor in his marriage from earliest times. Although he had barely come to know her spiritually, he was physically in love with his wife and quite jealous. He expected to know Kasturba's whereabouts every waking moment and soon required her to have his permission to go out of the house at all. Kasturba, used to having her own way, was not about to stand for this virtual imprisonment, and the couple quarreled bitterly.

The tension only heightened when Gandhi decided to tutor Kasturba in reading. Kasturba's illiteracy was typical in India at that time, as most women were not taught to read and write. Kasturba, like other women at that time, did not see the need to learn these skills because her life would be about cooking, cleaning, and children, rather than books. However, Gandhi persisted. He was still in high school, so he taught at night, against Kasturba's will. At the time, married couples of these young ages only spent part of their time living together. Gandhi claimed he spent no more than six months at the longest with his wife in a period of five years. Kasturba spent the balance of that time with her own parents. This on-and-off living arrangement and Kasturba's unwillingness to learn did not produce the desired results. Even into adulthood, Kasturba could only read and write rudimentary sentences in Gujarati, the Gandhis' native tongue.

STILL A BOY

The fact that Kasturba may have been more mature than her husband did not help matters, either, as women were expected to be servile and completely compliant to their husbands' will at that time. Before women's liberation in most parts of the world, women took a vow of obedience to their husbands during the marriage ceremony. Especially in such patriarchal societies as India, no husband's wish or order was to be questioned—only fulfilled. However, when Gandhi became a husband, he was still afraid of the dark and insisted that a light be left on at night, as he feared attacks from spirits or snakes.

He was also still quite timid at school and disliked adversity of any kind. If a teacher admonished him, he became mortified, and once, when he received corporal punishment, he cried—not from the discomfort that it caused, but from knowing that he had done wrong. He enjoyed walking but was not interested in physical sports. He hated cricket and gymnastics, although he had no choice in participating when the headmaster of his school made both mandatory. He had only one salvation: caring for his father, who was by that time bedridden.

Kaba had never recovered from the injuries he had suffered in the carriage accident while on his way to his sons' wedding. Each day, Gandhi rushed home after school to cheerfully tend his father. In fact, Gandhi always enjoyed caring for the sick or wounded, and had it not been for the family's expectation that he follow Kaba into political life, he might have opted to join the medical profession in some capacity.

Gandhi's lack of physical ability was supplanted by his intelligence. He was a good student and skipped a grade between his third and fourth years at the high school, but it may not have been the best course of action. By the fourth year or standard, all classes were conducted in English, with which he was not completely familiar. Geometry became especially difficult for him and although Gandhi thought his teacher was quite competent, he had difficulty following the concepts of the course. He considered falling back into the third standard, but his unwillingness to disappoint those who recommended him for promotion stopped him. Finally, when they came to Euclid's thirteenth proposition, the sea of knowledge parted for him.[7] From that time, he claimed that geometry was easy for him, although he did not have such an easy time with Sanskrit.

Nor did he have any early success at being a reformer. Gandhi was warned against his older brother's best friend, Sheikh Mehtab, not only by his family but also by his wife. Gandhi saw Mehtab as troubled but was convinced that he could change Mehtab's mischievous ways by setting a good example. This inability to change Mehtab became one of Gandhi's personal failures.

The Gandhis were vegetarians and, because of Putliba's beliefs and example, abstained from eating meat. Mehtab soon pointed out to young Mohan that the English, who ruled over their native land, were strong because they were carnivorous. He also pointed to many of their teachers, who had become enlightened to this fact. The educators were not only eating meat but also drinking wine, another forbidden pleasure. Mehtab said that the English were able to control India because they were stronger than Indians, and he kept prodding Gandhi to succumb to these so-called modern ways. Over time, Gandhi began to see the advantage. At this early age, he wanted to be stronger and, even then, to make India free. The boys began to eat meat secretly.

They went to a spot beside the river and for the first time in his life, Gandhi saw raw meat and, rather than the unleavened bread he was used to, yeast-baked bread from a bakery. On his first encounter, he tasted raw goat's meat, but it made him sick and he had to stop eating. Mehtab soon tempted Gandhi with cooked meat dishes and moved their eating sessions indoors to an inn with a cook and tables and chairs. Soon, Gandhi lost his aversion to bread and meat, and he and Mehtab met about six times over a one-year period to consume the forbidden foods.

But he could not handle the pressure of lying to his parents, even by omission. His mother would fix dinner, but as he had already eaten, he would neglect his food. When his mother asked why he was not eating, Gandhi would tell her he had an upset stomach. After tasting meat only a few times in his life, Gandhi made the vow never to eat meat again while his parents were still living. In fact, he never ate meat again for the rest of his life.

LIBERTY OR DEATH?

Another bad habit that Mehtab introduced Gandhi to was smoking. The coconspirators began by stealing butts left by Gandhi's uncle, but the pair soon stole coins, mainly from Gandhi's brother, and used them to buy Indian cigarettes. When money was not readily available, they smoked the stalks of porous plants, which was less than satisfying. The boys reveled in this disobedience and soon became indignant that they should need the permission of their parents to take pleasure in something involving their own bodies.

In an adolescent fit of pique, Gandhi and Mehtab decided to commit suicide by consuming fistfuls of datura, or jimsonweed, seeds, which in high doses can be fatal. When the time came, they set up a ritual camp in the jungle. Then, they lost their courage: Instead of taking enough seeds to kill them, they only took enough to make them sick. The two quickly decided that it was better to put up with a lack of independence than to be dead. From that time on, Gandhi never worried then when someone threatened to commit suicide, as he realized it was much easier to do than to say. He also stopped smoking.

In fact, Gandhi stopped all his wayward behavior. The guilt was too much for him, and he could not face his parents with the truth. Instead, he wrote a long letter to his father, and asked his forgiveness for all the wrongs he had done over this period. He was not afraid of a beating, only of disappointing the two people he still loved most in the world. When his father read the letter, rather than chastising the boy, he only cried. Gandhi wrote, "For a moment he closed his eyes in thought and then tore up the note."[8] Nothing more was said of the incident and no punishment was given. Gandhi's father seemed to know that the boy had punished himself enough and was satisfied with his vow never to sin again.

However, Gandhi's guilt would intensify. When Gandhi was 16 years old, his father was still confined to bed, suffering from what Gandhi called a fistula, which occurs when damaged tissues inside the body become infected and exhibit on the outside of the body or when damaged tissues come together and heal, rather than healing apart. It is not clear what type of fistula was involved in Kaba's case, but the injuries sustained in the carriage accident on the way to his sons' wedding were its cause. The only recourse to his ailment seemed to be an operation, and although one had been prepared, it was decided that Kaba was so weak that he would not survive the surgery.

During this time, Gandhi knew that Kaba's condition was grave. Kaba's brother Tulsidas had been called from Porbandar to sit with him, and Gandhi spent every waking hour at his father's bedside. Because the young man was exhausted, Gandhi's uncle told him to sleep for a while and that he would take charge of his brother for the night. Gandhi was reluctant, but the thought of communing with his wife swayed his resolve and he retired. Kasturba was already asleep when Gandhi entered the room, yet he awakened her for lovemaking. However, to mortification so great that it would follow him and his attitudes toward sex until the end of his days, a knock came to the door within 10 minutes. Kaba was dead.

Gandhi tortured himself with the knowledge that he was not present at his father's last moment, owing to the fact that he was in bed, having sex with his wife. To add to his moral dilemma, Kasturba was pregnant with their first child at the time, and the baby was born only four days later. It lived only a few days and then it also died. Gandhi would never forgive himself for his inability to hold his carnal passions in check. One incident had changed his life forever.

NOTES

1. Arun and Sunanda Gandhi, *The Forgotten Woman: the Untold Story of Kastur, Wife of Mahatma Gandhi* (Huntsville, AR: Ozark Mountain Publishers, 1998), p. 6.

2. Mohandas K. Gandhi, *An Autobiography: The Story of My Experiments with Truth* (*Satyanāprayogo athavā ātmakathā*, 1927, translated by Mahadev Desai; reprint Boston: Beacon Press, 1993), p. 3–4.

3. Dr. C.S. Shah, "Shravana," *IndiaNest.com*, http://www.boloji.com/hinduism/ramayana/02.htm.

4. Gandhi, *An Autobiography*, p. 7.

5. Gandhi, *An Autobiography*, p. 11.

6. Gandhi, *An Autobiography*, p. 11.

7. Assuming he was discussing Book One of Euclid's *Elements*, that proposition is as follows: If a straight line stands on a straight line, then it makes either two right angles or angles whose sum equals two right angles.

8. Gandhi, *An Autobiography*, p. 27.

Chapter 2

BECOMING AN ENGLISH GENTLEMAN

In November 1887, Gandhi traveled to Ahmedabad, the largest city in Kathiawar peninsula and the capital of Gujarat. He was set to take his matriculation examination, which would determine his readiness for higher education. It was the first time that Gandhi had been away from provincial Rajkot, and Ahmedabad must have seemed enormous to him. The largest city he had visited until that time had been Porbandar, with a population around 15,000. Ahmedabad's population was more than 100,000 at the time, and the architecture was much more sophisticated. Gandhi saw regal palaces of marble where rajahs (princes) lived, bungalows inhabited by British nationals, lush gardens, and many sophisticated people. Among the population were Parsis, Jews, and Christians, mingling with the majority sect of Hindus. Whereas some people were elegantly dressed in stiff collars and formal turbans, the Hindu merchants dressed in the traditional informal wear of India like *kurtas*—long, stand-up collar, long-sleeved shirts, worn with *pijamo* trousers—or dhotis—and bare chests. To the young Gandhi, this eclectic mixture of sights, sounds, and smells must have been overwhelming.

However, his academic performance throughout his later high school years had been under par, and he was anxious about doing well on the matriculation exam. His passing grade was important to the family. From early on, Kaba had intended that his youngest son assume a political role, thereby becoming the main support for the extended family. This responsibility weighed heavily on Gandhi. He managed to pass, but barely. His marks were only 247.5 out of 625; that he passed at all was an achievement.

Only 800 of the 3,000 students who took the examination had made a passing grade.

Soon after returning from Ahmedabad, Gandhi applied to Samaldas College in Bhavnagar, some 90 miles southeast of Rajkot, and around the same time learned that Kasturba was pregnant for the second time. She was eager for the birth of a healthy child and accompanied her mother-in-law to the temple every day, hoping for the delivery of a healthy son. Indian girls were still considered a burden to their families, as they brought no income, only another mouth to feed. Kasturba's sister-in-law, Nandkunwarba, the wife of Laxmidas, was also pregnant at the same time, and each wondered who would have the first son and heir. Gandhi left home, hoping that his second child would thrive in its mother's womb.

The college term began in January 1888. To get to Bhavnagar, Gandhi traveled by train to reach his rented apartment, where he would live alone for the first time in his life. The solitude made him unhappy and caused him to be lackadaisical with his schoolwork. He found it hard to grasp what the professors were teaching because he was still uncomfortable with the English language. He quickly lost interest in his studies and his grades faltered. By the end of the first term, he returned to Rajkot, not expecting his studies to continue.

Gandhi's personal failure was devastating for the family. After Kaba died leaving little inheritance, Laxmidas became responsible for the security of his entire extended family. Hopes that Gandhi would graduate from college and help the family had been dashed. In desperation, the family called upon Mavji Dave Joshi, an old friend and advisor, to help them decide their future.

Joshi made little of Gandhi's failure at college and said that Gandhi should have a proper education to enter the legal profession, which would lead to success in politics, reminding them that another young man who had returned with an English education and excellent prospects for the future. Joshi's own son had gone to London to complete law school, and Joshi assured the family that his son would provide guidance for Gandhi while he was away.

Gandhi was not excited about the possibility of becoming a lawyer. Instead, he hoped that Joshi would entertain his hopes of becoming a health professional, but Laxmidas forbade it, and said, "Father intended you for the bar."[1]

Putliba balked at the idea of sending Gandhi to England at all. Not only would she lose her favorite son, but she worried that if he did come back, he would be corrupted and polluted by eating meat, drinking wine, and consorting with bad women. Her solution was to seek a higher authority. She told Gandhi that since Kaba's brother Tulsidas was now the elder of the family, Gandhi would have to travel to Porbandar to seek Tulsidas's permission. Laxmidas worried about the expense of sending his brother to England and told Gandhi to speak with Frederick Lely, the British representative, and plead for a scholarship.

LEARNING TO BE A MAN

Before Gandhi left for Porbandar, Kasturba delivered a healthy baby boy. Much rejoicing followed within the family because a new Gandhi heir had arrived. Laxmidas and Nandkunwarba's baby had arrived earlier, but it had been a girl. Little celebrating took place at that time, but with the birth of a boy, great feasts were prepared, all the relatives were alerted, and everyone rejoiced. Six days later, after a purification ceremony, Kasturba emerged from the birthing room for a momentous and solemn event. According to Hindu belief, their Lord decides a baby's destiny on the sixth day of his or her life. Also on this day, the child receives a name. Gandhi and Kasturba's son would be named Harilal, meaning "the Son of God."[2]

Soon after, Gandhi left Rajkot for Porbandar, via bullock cart and camel. On his arrival in Porbandar, he first visited his uncle and told him of Joshi's recommendation. Yet, his uncle was reluctant to give permission for Gandhi to go to England. Like Putliba, he saw trouble for Gandhi, and asked, "At the threshold of death, how dare I give you permission to go to England, to cross the seas?"[3] Yet, he told Gandhi that he would not stand in his way and that it was his mother's position on the matter that was important. He refused to give him a letter of recommendation to Lely, however, which made Gandhi realize that his uncle would not stop him from leaving India—but he would not help Gandhi, either.

Without his uncle's blessing, Gandhi wrote a letter to Lely, asking for an appointment and, because of the Gandhi family's good reputation, an appointment was set. However, when Gandhi arrived, Lely was not waiting for him but ascending a staircase. Even so, Gandhi showed obeisance by bowing with his palms folded and then proceeded to explain his presence. But before he could finish his story, Lely cut him off. "Pass your B.A. first, then see me. No help can be given you now," he said.[4] It is often remarked that Lely had no idea that he had just rebuffed the one man who would later bring down the British Empire in India.

Gandhi returned to Rajkot, with new ideas about financing his English education through the sale of Kasturba's jewelry. Laxmidas, trusting in Joshi's advice, agreed to this bargain. As a wife, and thereby secondary to her husband's will, Kasturba had no say in the matter, but she was a strong girl and probably not keen on the idea. Still, she could not complain.

Putliba wanted to consult another family advisor before giving her final word on the matter and invited Becharji Swami's opinion. Swami told her that he would ask Gandhi to take three vows—that he would not touch wine, women, or meat—and with these oaths, Putliba should capitulate and allow Gandhi to make the journey. After Gandhi took the vows, Putliba reluctantly granted her permission.

Because not many in Rajkot left for overseas journeys, a big party was held for Gandhi's send-off on August 10, 1888. Although friends and relatives supported the young man's decision and gathered to see him off and wish him well, his mother was still distraught at the idea of losing her son to England. Gandhi wrote, "I did not weep, even though my heart was breaking."[5]

Gandhi also found it hard to leave his wife and baby. He took Kasturba into a separate room to say good-bye. He kissed her and she whispered her futile wish for him not to leave, but there was no reversing his decision. Laxmidas had already purchased the tickets for the first leg of the journey to Bombay (modern Mumbai), on which he would accompany Gandhi. They would stay with their sister Raliatben and her husband. Before leaving, Gandhi gathered his high-school friends around him and made a short speech: "I hope that some of you will follow in my footsteps and after you return from England you will work whole-heartedly for big reforms in India."[6]

OUTSIDE THE NORM

On reaching Bombay, Gandhi and Laxmidas found out that a ship had just been sunk off the coast of Africa, and Gandhi was advised not to attempt the journey across the Indian Ocean until November, when the monsoon season would be over. Laxmidas left Gandhi with some friends and gave his money to Raliatben's husband for safekeeping. The time in Bombay dragged on for Gandhi, who was anxious to get to England, but it was punctuated by one unfortunate event.

Almost as soon as Laxmidas had left to return to India, the Modh Bania Caste leadership became incensed over Gandhi's impending trip to England. No Modh Bania had ever been abroad, and a caste meeting was called to discuss the matter. The elders told Gandhi that going abroad was against his religion and that it was not possible to go to England without eating and drinking with Europeans. Gandhi disagreed. He told the Sheth, the headman of the community, that he did not think it was against his religion and that he fully intended to go to England to pursue further studies.[7] When asked if he would disobey an order of the caste, Gandhi replied, "I think the caste should not interfere in the matter."[8] This incensed the Sheth to such a degree that he swore at Gandhi and proclaimed, "This boy shall be treated as an outcast from today."[9] Anyone who even dared to see Gandhi off at the dock was subject to a fine.

In light of the caste's action, there was no time to lose. Gandhi worried that the elders would get to his brother and put an end to his dreams of England, so he consulted with friends and found that the *S.S. Clyde* was leaving port on September 4. He planned to be among its passengers and quickly wired home to ask his brother's permission to sail, which was granted. Then, Gandhi ran into another obstacle: His brother-in-law would not relinquish the money Laxmidas had entrusted to him for Gandhi, referring to the caste's decision. This did not stop Gandhi. He borrowed money from a friend in Bombay and told the man that his brother would repay the loan because there was no restriction on Gandhi's brother-in-law returning the money to Laxmidas and Laxmidas satisfying the debt.

With part of the money, Gandhi set off to buy appropriate clothing for England. He purchased a sport jacket and a necktie and was then commended to the care of Sergeant Tryambakrai Mazmudar, a *vakil* (a legal practitioner) from Junagadh. The older and more sophisticated Mazmudar would be Gandhi's guide and protector for the eight-week voyage. Although Mazmudar was some help, Gandhi still had to fare on his own most of the time, and he felt alienated from the other second-class passengers, who were mainly British returning to England. He was too shy to meet others and had a difficult time speaking English. He spent most of the cruise in his cabin and was lucky enough not to fall victim to seasickness.

Gandhi did have a conversation with one English gentleman, but only because the man spoke to Gandhi first. They talked about Gandhi's shyness, and the Englishman encouraged Gandhi to come to the dinner table in the evening. He also asked what Gandhi's diet was like, and when he suggested that Gandhi would need to eat meat in England to survive the cold, Gandhi recounted his vow, saying that he would rather go back to India than to break it. Later, he even asked his English friend to give him a certificate stating that Gandhi had not eaten meat or taken even a sip of wine during the entire cruise, which the Englishman did.

After putting into port at Aden, Yemen; Port Said, Egypt; Brindisi, Italy; the Isle of Malta; and Gibraltar at the tip of Spain, the *S.S. Clyde* reached its final destination on October 28, 1888, at Southampton, England. At the time, London was the largest city in the world, doubling the size of either New York or Paris, and it was home to about 200 Indians, studying either business or law. The year 1888 was also the time of the Whitechapel murderer, who would later come to be known as Jack the Ripper.

A WHITE ELEPHANT LANDS IN THE NEW WORLD

Gandhi had kept a white flannel suit for the momentous occasion of landing in England and soon realized he was immediately out of place. During Victorian times, white was never worn after the end of summer, but this was not the only culture shock Gandhi would encounter. He had never seen electric lights and elevators frightened him, for example. Gandhi had to adjust to the new culture and try to appear civilized at the same time. Changes in his manners and ways of thinking had to be made quickly, as fitting in was very important to him.

Gandhi arrived in London with four notes of introduction. He had been advised to stay at the Victoria Hotel and traveled there with Sergeant Mazmudar, after arranging to have his belongings delivered to the inn. However, the shipping company could not get his things to him for two days, as he had arrived on a weekend. In the late nineteenth century, no one worked on the Sabbath. Gandhi was mortified that he had to walk around London for such an extended period, sticking out like a white elephant.

Soon Gandhi met Sir Pherozeshah Mehta, an influential Bombay businessman and family acquaintance. The man was cordial but Gandhi sensed his amusement over the white flannel suit in the midst of autumn. He was also annoyed by Gandhi's curiosity and lack of sophistication. At one point, Gandhi picked up Mehta's beaver felt top hat and stroked the fur the wrong way. Mehta, experienced in English civility, gently rebuked him, saying, "Do not touch other people's things. Do not ask questions as we usually do in India on first acquaintance; do not talk loudly; never address people as 'sir' whilst speaking to them as we do in India"[10] and continued on with many other suggestions. Gandhi called this his first lesson in European etiquette.

Another suggestion of Mehta's was that Gandhi move from the hotel where he was staying to a room with a private family, which would be more economical, but Gandhi deferred this decision. He was pathetically homesick and wrote that he cried every night, especially because he missed his mother. To make matters worse, he contracted ringworm, a fungal infection that can affect the scalp, nails, feet, or entire body, yet has nothing to do with actual worms. The name comes from the mark that the fungus leaves on the skin, which appears as a raised red ring. Gandhi claimed to have gotten the disease on the boat, when he used soap to clean himself. He could have gotten the fungus from someone who had used the soap before him, but more likely, he became infected by proximity to another infected person. Mehta, who came to visit his hotel room, told Gandhi to apply acetic acid to the spots, and Gandhi complained that it stung him to the point of tears. Mehta also insisted that Gandhi change quarters, saying that to experience English life, he needed to live with an English family. While searching for the proper family, Mehta planned to set Gandhi up with another Indian friend in the district of Richmond, who would round off Gandhi's rural Indian demeanor to suit English society.

Gandhi's new living companion was kind and treated him like a brother. The man practiced English with Gandhi until Gandhi became more comfortable using the language. He also encouraged Gandhi to read newspapers. *The Daily News, The Daily Telegraph,* and *The Pall Mall Gazette* were Gandhi's papers of choice, and diligent reading helped improve his facility with reading in English.

Gandhi's vegetarianism was also out of place, and he existed on a meager diet of oatmeal for breakfast and boiled spinach, bread, butter, and jam for lunch and dinner. Although he was starving, he would not break the vow he made to his mother not to eat meat, no matter how much his host tried to persuade him. Gandhi remained adamant, allowing the quest for a perfect diet to take a major part in his life.

After Gandhi spent a month with his Indian mentor, Mehta arranged to place Gandhi with a widowed landlady in the London borough of West Kensington. She was sympathetic to Gandhi's vow of not eating meat, but he thought her food unexciting. The vegetables were not cooked with salt and spices as Gandhi was used to having in India, and he thought the food had no flavor. He was starving. He could not eat enough bread to sustain him, and milk, which he could drink and which gave him a measure of sustenance, was never served with meals in his new home. To save his health, Gandhi set off on a quest to find a vegetarian restaurant somewhere in London and walked 10–12 miles in search of a suitable eating establishment each day. Eventually, he found a restaurant called *The Central,* where he enjoyed his first filling meal since arriving in England. He also acquired a book at the restaurant, titled *Salt's Plea for Vegetarianism* by Henry Stephens Salt, a vegetarian and animal rights activist, which Gandhi read as voraciously as he had eaten his first English vegetarian meal. For the first time, he saw the benefits of a vegetarian life, making his eating habits a choice, not a product of mother's will. Gandhi would remain a conscientious vegetarian throughout his life.

LEARNING SOPHISTICATION

With his eating problem solved, another of Gandhi's ongoing pursuits was learning to become an English gentleman. He bought new English day wear and a stovepipe hat, and for the evening, a suit with a cutaway coat, which was made on Bond Street, renowned for its tasteful, classic men's fashions. To complete his outfit, Gandhi asked his brother to send him a golden double chain for his watch. Although mirrors were scarce in India, Gandhi had the luxury of spending a great deal of time in front of them in England, making sure that his hair was parted properly and that his tie was on straight.

Appearance was only one aspect of Gandhi's infatuation with English society. He was also encouraged to take lessons in French, dancing, and elocution so that he would speak English properly. However, he proved to be a terrible dancer and soon resigned that pursuit to play the violin. On the whole, Gandhi's quest for Western civility did not last long. After only three months, he realized that he required only what he needed to get into legal studies, and the rest would come as he continued to live in England—or not, and though societal assimilation became less important to him, he continued to dress in the English fashion for many years.

Gandhi's intellectual decision had some basis in hard reality, as finances had become a concern. He kept a strict accounting of every farthing spent each day; he soon realized that if he wanted to stay in England as long as was necessary for him to finish his studies, he would have to cut his living expenses by half. Boarding with the English landlady and her family was comfortable but expensive. He had to pay not only the weekly rent, but for other civilities, like taking family members out to dinner or attending parties, which required a small token for the host. To economize, he moved to a small room that was convenient to his legal society: the Inns of Court, which were situated in central London and a walking distance of half an hour. He enrolled on November 6, 1888. Now situated to his satisfaction, he could concentrate on preparing for the bar.

Gandhi's chosen Inn of Court of the four existing societies was The Honorable Society of the Inner Temple, the group most favored by Indian students. Founded centuries before Gandhi became a member, the Inns of Court have the exclusive right of educating students for admission to the bar, which the British designate as being "called to the bar." The societies are more like clubs than schools, in that old masters come to gather with new legal hopefuls through dinners, seminars, lectures, moot courts, and debates to prepare them to navigate in court. But one friend suggested to Gandhi that these gatherings would simply not be enough. He suggested that Gandhi pass the London Matriculation, equivalent to an examination for a Bachelor of Arts degree to shore his academic background.

One requirement for the exam was the study of Latin and a modern language, for which Gandhi chose French, because he had already begun to study the language. A science course was also compulsory, and he chose Heat and Light because he thought it would be an easy subject. He joined a private matriculation class to prepare for the exam, only five months away.

Gandhi thought that he was still spending too much of his available cash, so he moved once again to smaller accommodations. In this one-room apartment, Gandhi now used a stove he bought to cook meals of porridge and cocoa for breakfast and bread and cocoa for dinner. His frugality helped to ensure that Gandhi would be able to stay in London for as long as was needed for his studies. Gandhi studied for the college equivalency exam and the regular curriculum at the Inner Temple at the same time. His chosen path of the simple life gave him more time to concentrate, and his hard work and diligent budgeting paid off in June of 1890 when he passed the London Matriculation.

During this time, Gandhi continued to be involved with his vegetarianism. He read more books on the subject and joined the London Vegetarian Society. He quickly subscribed to its weekly journal, *The Vegetarian*, and not long afterward found himself a member of the society's executive committee. In his dietetic studies, he came to learn that in England there were three definitions of meat. The first analysis included only the flesh of birds and animals as meat. Those subscribing to this definition ate fish and eggs. The second idea of vegetarianism excluded the flesh of all living creatures, and those who followed this philosophy eschewed fish but consumed eggs. The third variation excluded not only the flesh of all living beings, but also their products, such as milk and eggs. During this time in his life, Gandhi upheld the second definition of vegetarianism, although he would later change his ways to exclude even the products of living things.

PORTENTS OF THE FUTURE

Vegetarianism also led Gandhi to make his first public speech. He and Sergeant Mazmudar were staying with a vegetarian family in Ventnor on the Isle of Wight, where they also met Howard Williams, the author of *The Ethics of Diet: A Catena of Authorities Deprecatory of the Practice of Flesh-Eating*. In his book, Williams referred to eating meat as butchery and presented the many famous vegetarians in history, including Plato, Ovid, Pythagoras, Pope, Voltaire, Rousseau, Shelley, Schopenhauer, and

Thoreau. Williams invited Gandhi and Mazmudar to speak at a meeting to promote vegetarianism, and Gandhi agreed.

Reading a prewritten speech seemed acceptable to Gandhi. He thought that to speak extemporaneously at that point would have been a disaster. Although he had prepared an oration, he could not even eke out the words to read it to his audience. His vision blurred and his body shook, and Sergeant Mazmudar had to read the speech for him. Gandhi's ideas were well received, but he was mortified by his lack of courage. In later years, Gandhi came to view his shyness as an asset. He claimed that it taught him economy with words and gave him the habit of restraining his thoughts. He wrote, "And I can now give myself the certificate that a thoughtless word hardly ever escapes my tongue or pen."[11]

Gandhi would come to be seen in an ethereal light as he moved through life. Goodness just seemed to emanate from his persona. Yet, in his younger years, as noted previously, he was not always so sanctified. While in England, he hid the fact that he was married. He did so because he was lonely and knew that if he disclosed the fact that he had a wife, he would naturally have been left out of many social engagements.

He developed a relationship with a widow in Brighton, another seaside resort on the southeast coast of England, who took a personal vow to find Gandhi a suitable partner. She owned a hotel, and realizing that Gandhi could not navigate the hotel restaurant's billet, she offered her assistance in discerning which dishes would be suitable to Gandhi's vegetarian palate. This led to a long-term friendship and dinner each Sunday at the widow's home. Often, these dinners would include young ladies whom the matchmaking widow thought might hit it off with the young Indian barrister-in-training.

Gandhi enjoyed these Sundays and his conversations with young feminine friends, but eventually, the deception overwhelmed him with shame. He ached to admit the truth and offered a long written apology to the widow, confessing his marriage. When she not only accepted his apology, but insisted that the Sunday dinners continue, Gandhi was much relieved.

Another of Gandhi's pursuits while in England was the quest for spirituality. Although he was raised Hindu, his mother had influences from the Parsi faith that he found interesting, and other philosophies also attracted him. He wanted to study each one before making any final choices. In the second half of 1890, he began study of the Hindu *Bhagavad Gita*, also known as the *Gitopanishad* or simply, the *Gita*. This highly respected story of Indian wisdom is told by the Lord Krishna to his disciple Arjuna and is seen as a guide to self-realization. A translation of

Chapter 8, Text 8 reads, "One should meditate upon the Supreme Person as the one who knows everything, as He who is the oldest, who is the controller, who is smaller than the smallest, who is the maintainer of everything, who is beyond all material conception, who is inconceivable, and who is always a person. He is luminous like the sun, and He is transcendental, beyond this material nature."[12] This work affected Gandhi profoundly and became his "bible" of truth.

Gandhi also became fascinated by Theosophy, a belief that synthesizes religion, science, and philosophy and leans heavily on Eastern wisdom. Two brothers who were Theosophists befriended Gandhi, and the three often had intense philosophical discussions. Ironically, they had introduced Gandhi to the *Gita*, although he was brought up in the Hindu faith. They also presented him with other books of self-realization, including *The Light of Asia* by Sir Edwin Arnold. As their guest at the Blavatsky Lodge, the home of Theosophy in London, he was introduced to Madame Helena Petrovna Blavatsky, the first Russian woman to become a naturalized American citizen and founder of the Theosophical Society in New York in 1875. He also met Annie Besant, a devout Theosophist and someone Gandhi would meet again in the future.

FINALIZING HIS TASK

While at the lodge, Gandhi was encouraged to join the Theosophist movement, but he declined, owing to his limited knowledge of Hinduism and his ongoing investigation of other philosophies. He subsequently studied the Bible. He disliked the Old Testament, claiming that the book nearly put him to sleep, especially the book of Numbers. Yet, he relished the New Testament, the story of Jesus Christ. The Sermon on the Mount was the most powerful passage for him, and Jesus's message went straight to his heart.

Jesus's life encouraged Gandhi to read the lives of other great religious leaders, such as Mohammed, and even the life of Charles Bradlaugh, a confirmed atheist and the founder of England's National Secular Society, which claimed that belief in supernaturalism was based in ignorance and deleterious to progress. Gandhi and 3,000 others attended Bradlaugh's funeral on February 3, 1891. However, after hearing another atheist heckle a clergyman while at the funeral, Gandhi solidified his disdain for atheism and his faith in prayer and worship. "It is no exaggeration to say that [faith and prayer] alone are real, all else is unreal."[13]

Throughout this time, Gandhi was preparing for his legal exams, and in Gandhi's time, two conditions had to be fulfilled before his call to the bar was formal. First, he had to "keep terms," which meant he had to attend six dinners out of the 24 held in a semester. This did not necessarily mean eating during the dinners, only that one had to be present and to listen closely to the wisdom imparted through one's elder associates.

The second requirement for being formally called to the bar was that Gandhi pass a legal examination, although he remarked that the exams had practically no value. Gandhi studied hard in pursuit of a passing grade. He read Roman law in Latin and thought that it served him in good stead later in his career. He also took nine months to read the Common Law of England, and during the same time period, he read several other law books pertaining to different aspects of the law. Three written tests—in Roman law, English Common Law, and Equity—were included in the exam, which he passed on June 10, 1891, although he still did not feel adequately prepared to practice law. Of all students who took the exam, 95 percent to 99 percent passed, and Gandhi said it was very difficult to fail. Even so unsure of himself, he enrolled in the High Court on June 11, thereby becoming a fully warranted lawyer.

Gandhi did not waste any time, once his goal had been achieved. He had spent three years in England, away from his family, and he wanted to see them. Yet, aside from the pleasure a reunion would bring, he would miss the civility of England and was not completely excited about returning to India. In addition to forgoing the enhanced sophistication to which he had become accustomed, there were the enormous expectations of the family. He had to rush home and contribute to his family's support and thought he had little choice but to sail for India at his earliest opportunity. In a parting interview in the *Vegetarian*, Gandhi remarked that he was sad to leave England—"Who would not be?"[14] On June 12, 1891, he boarded the *S.S. Assam* at Southampton and set sail for India.

NOTES

1. Quoted in Gandhi, *An Autobiography*, p. 36.
2. Arun and Sunanda Gandhi, *The Forgotten Woman*, 36.
3. Quoted in Gandhi, *An Autobiography*, p. 37.
4. Quoted in Gandhi, *An Autobiography*, p. 38.
5. Quoted in Arun and Sunanda Gandhi, *The Forgotten Woman*, pp. 37–38.
6. Quoted in Geoffrey Ashe, *Gandhi: a Biography* (New York: Stein and Day, 1968; reprint Cooper Square Press, 2000), p. 15.
7. A term afforded to an influential businessperson.
8. Gandhi, *An Autobiography*, p. 40.
9. Gandhi, *An Autobiography*, p. 40.

10. Quoted in Gandhi, *An Autobiography*, p. 44.

11. Gandhi, *An Autobiography*, p. 62

12. *An Introduction to the Bhagavad-Gita*, Chapter 8, Text 8 (translated by Bhaktivedanta Swami Prabhupada, 2005), http://www.bhagavad-gita.us/bhagavad-gita-8–8.htm.

13. Gandhi, *An Autobiography*, p. 72.

14. Stanley Wolpert, *Gandhi's Passion: The Life and Legacy of Mahatma Gandhi* (New York: Oxford University Press, 2001), p. 27.

Chapter 3

INDIA FROM A DIFFERENT POINT OF VIEW

Gandhi's journey back to India was horribly unpleasant. As it was monsoon season, the seas were choppy, and nearly everyone on board the ship became ill—except Gandhi. He found the stormy seas to be a metaphor for his emotions at that time. Not only his family, but exile from his caste was on his mind, added to the uncertainty of practicing law in India. His burden was considerable, but even more torment would hit him immediately on his arrival in Bombay.

His brother Laxmidas met Gandhi as he disembarked, but it was Putliba, his mother, that Gandhi was anxious to see. He was closer to her than anyone in the world, including his wife. The time away from his mother had been excruciating and although the brothers were offered lodging at Sir Pherozeshah Mehta's house in Bombay for a while, Gandhi was anxious to return to Rajkot and immediately asked Laxmidas about their mother on landing. Laxmidas dodged the question until they were settled in for the night but finally admitted that their mother had died while Gandhi was in London. The family had discussed whether to impart the sad news to Gandhi at the time of Putliba's death but had decided that Gandhi could have done nothing but grieve alone. "My grief was even greater than over my father's death," he wrote.[1] Yet Gandhi wore the stiff upper lip he had developed in England and continued life as though nothing had happened. He was aware of the expectations his family placed on him and maintained a seriousness of purpose.

Laxmidas was particularly eager for Gandhi's success and advised Gandhi that it was imperative for him to return to the caste first, adding that it was his mother's last wish that Gandhi do so. Caste members for and against

Gandhi had turned the situation into a major conflict, and it had already begun to affect the family adversely. Putliba's funeral was curtailed because of Gandhi's excommunication, and several of their family members and friends could not attend. Even seeing her family was difficult for Kasturba, as they were bound to keep up the appearance of denying any Gandhi core family member solace. She had to sneak visits to them when there was no chance of discovery. It was predictable that Gandhi would get no business until the dispute was settled.

Following prescribed rituals, Laxmidas took Gandhi to Nasik, Maharashtra, 187 kilometers (roughly 116 miles) from Bombay, to the sacred Godavari River, one of the seven sacred rivers in India. Laxmidas bathed his brother in the river, and then the pair continued their pilgrimage to Rajkot. A ceremonial dinner had been planned for the caste elders there, where a shirtless Gandhi would serve them. Although Gandhi thought that the ritual was inane, he followed through for the good of his family. To have treated him as a family member would have caused their own excommunication, and although they had prepared to welcome Gandhi and ignore his exile, Gandhi could not allow it. The excommunication would be rescinded once the elders accepted food from him and he paid a hefty fine. However, Gandhi would never have loyalty to the caste system. In his eyes, all men were equal, and he would come to unsettle such ancient belief systems in the future.

Gandhi had developed his passion for reformation while in England, as exhibited by his undertaking of the vegetarian cause, and his relish in changing things for the better did not diminish when he returned to India. Suspecting this might happen, Laxmidas had made some preparations for his brother's return, such as substituting fine china and pottery for the family's traditional brass *vadkas* (bowls) and *thalis* (plates). He also brought chairs into the house so they could dine at a table, rather than eat while sitting on the floor. But Kasturba was unprepared. Just seeing her "new" husband was shocking. Both husband and wife had matured, but she had not left their Indian province, whereas Gandhi had become a gentleman of the world. She hardly recognized him.

Gandhi continued the mission to make things at the Gandhi household more Western. He wanted first to prepare his son's mind, so he began to home school him and his cousins. He tried to further Anglicize other members of his family as well: He set them to eating oatmeal for breakfast and drinking cocoa, rather than tea or coffee. And although the family had taken to wearing boots or shoes, rather than sandals, Gandhi completed the Western fashion by encouraging them to dress more like Europeans. He insisted that even the children no longer go barefoot and kept them on a strict regimen of walking and calisthenics each day. He was determined that they would grow up strong, like Westerners.

But when Gandhi extended his zeal for all that was English and insisted on resuming Kasturba's reading lessons at night, she was apathetic. Her lack of interest in mental pursuits, along with her incomprehension of his heightened station in life rankled Gandhi, and he persisted with her education, to her dismay. Other aspects of their relationship did not change, either. His old jealousies returned when he realized what a beauty he had married, and he continued to accuse her of cheating, without basis. The marriage began to falter.

NOT AT ALL PREPARED

The biggest problem with Gandhi's return home, however, was that he was not ready to be a lawyer. Although he had studied Roman and Common Law, he knew little of Hindu or Muslim law and thought of himself as less capable than a law clerk, the profession of Laxmidas. Still, he would be expected to charge fees that were considerably higher than his brother charged, simply because he was an English-trained barrister. The conundrum perplexed Gandhi. Charging such high prices without the skill to back the fees caused Gandhi to struggle emotionally. The debt he was expected to repay continued to haunt him. Rather than make a quick decision, he did nothing.

Kasturba, no longer the meek young girl she was when he left for England, chastised Gandhi for his inactivity and reminded him of his obligation, although she had never been so assertive before. Gandhi was indignant and, the next day, banished her to her parents' home in Porbandar. Kasturba did not take this as punishment but hoped that it would help Gandhi to examine his future. She saw herself as a distraction for him at that time, rather than inspiration, and knew that her husband would find his way back to her. The couple was separated for less than a month, and in that time, Gandhi had decided to accept Kasturba for who she was, to give her no further lessons that she did not want, and to abandon his suspicious and querulous nature. Kasturba, in turn, vowed to be more sympathetic to her husband's stresses.

The pressure on the marriage renewed when Gandhi was advised by friends to live near the high court for a while, and he and his brothers decided that he should moved to Bombay, where there would be more opportunity to learn, gain court experience, and earn money. He determined to leave Kasturba and Harilal in Rajkot to save expenses but assured his wife that she and the child might later join him. Being an obedient Hindu wife, Kasturba assented but did not tell him she suspected that she was pregnant for a third time. She did not want to upset him once the decision had been made. Knowing he had fathered another child might have increased Gandhi's guilt to a level he could not have borne. He languished in enormous guilt, stemming from many situations, such as knowing he had been with his wife while his father died, that he had lost his first son, that he had been in England when his mother died, and that he had to separate from his family to make a career, once again. He was emotionally miserable but knew what he had to do to survive.

Gandhi found a way to shelve the burden temporarily and, with high hopes, set up an apartment in the Girgaum section of Bombay. The living quarters included a cook named Ravishankar. The man's personal grooming habits were deplorable to Gandhi, as Ravishankar rinsed his body with water but used no soap, and his clothes were always dirty. Even worse, the man could not cook, causing Gandhi to don his familiar mantle of teacher. He spent many hours with Ravishankar, teaching him vegetarian cooking, but Ravishankar refused to maintain proper hygiene, either personally or in the kitchen.

Even a dirty cook added to Gandhi's expense and further fueled his mission to become a financial success. He began to study Indian law, and although his brother and other friends tried to get him cases, he knew he was not ready to handle them. One friend told him that it often took five to seven years before a barrister could get regular work in Bombay, so he took the first small case that was offered, but there was a catch. He was advised that he would have to pay a gratuity to the person who found the case for him. Gandhi refused, although other legal professionals encouraged him to pay the tip, saying he would get no work if he did not work inside the system. Yet Gandhi was adamant. He did not pay and got the case anyway, his fee for which was minimal.

However, it would come to pass that Gandhi would not keep the money he had been advanced. When it came time to cross-examine the plaintiff's witness, Gandhi became tongue-tied. His knees shook and he had to sit down and tell his client that he could not continue. He returned the payment and advised his client to hire an experienced lawyer. Gandhi would not return to court for a long time, but he did get another legal assignment that did not involve a courtroom appearance.

A farmer's lands had been confiscated in Porbandar, and Gandhi prepared his petition to the court for their restoration. On inspection by other friends in the legal profession, the appeal was found to be acceptable. This small victory afforded him the confidence he needed to pursue further business, as long as it did not require a court appearance.

NEW RESPONSIBILITY, OLD PROBLEM

To add to Gandhi's stresses, he received a letter from Laxmidas, telling him that he was about to be a father again. News of a second child was worth rejoicing over, but the addition to his family also added to the dilemma of not being able to earn a living. Another mouth to feed only heightened Gandhi's already loaded sense of guilt and frustration. He knew that he had to find a better way to make money because the legal profession was not supplying the needed income. Preparing documents would not support him or help him to attain acumen in the courts, so when he spied an advertisement for an English teacher at a Bombay high school, he applied for the position.

Gandhi was fervent about medicine and teaching but had become a lawyer. He was happy to have found a way to take on one of his interests, if only as an aside. Yet, when Gandhi had his interview with the school administrator, he was denied the job. Although he had passed the Matriculation Examination, he did not have a degree. Gandhi pleaded with the administrator that he had not only passed the Matriculation Examination, but also passed with Latin as his second language, but his arguments were to no avail. The high school required a bona fide degree, and that was the end of his aspirations of becoming a teacher.

With no way to support himself completely, Gandhi and Laxmidas decided that his only recourse was to return to Rajkot. Laxmidas thought that he could funnel some document drafting work to his brother, and Gandhi could move back in with the family, saving the expense of a second household. So, after only six months, Gandhi left Bombay. He returned to Rajkot, still unsure of himself and unprepared to practice his profession.

Gandhi's excellent drafting skills brought him about 300 rupees per month in Rajkot; however, he did have to capitulate to his staunch refusal of not paying commissions. Every barrister in Rajkot paid these fees to the clerks, without exception, and he decided to follow the norm, hoping to acquire more business. But around the time Gandhi was making a reasonable living, his brother presented him with a conundrum.

Laxmidas had taken a position as advisor to the crown prince of Porbandar via his uncle Tulsidas's influence. It had come to the attention of British officials that the prince, who had by then become the Raja of Porbandar, had taken some of the crown jewels from the state treasury without proper permission of the British agent, whose job it was to protect state assets from usurpation by local royalty. It had long been tacitly recognized that the local potentates would have reign in their respective territories, as long as they did not interfere with British suzerain power.

The British had acquired this hold over centuries. On December 31, 1600, Queen Elizabeth granted a charter to the English East India Trading Company, which established its first trading post at Surat in Gujarat. To the company, India was a mercantile venture, and its politics and religion were of no concern. They traded in tea, coffee, and cotton; expanded to coal and iron mining; and began construction of India's railway with little interest in changing the people's ways. By 1857, a group of Indians rebelled over the outsiders' control of their land in the Sepoy Rebellion or the Indian Rebellion of 1857–58. This war drove the East India Trading Company into virtual bankruptcy, and all the company's holdings in India and its debts were assumed by the British government. In turn, England made India a Crown Colony, with English Parliament taking over its governance and administration. A British cabinet member, the Secretary of the State for India, was the Indian Viceroy, under whom were the British agents in each Indian prince's court. These agents were the de facto rulers of the territories, though local rulers maintained the guise of control.

When the Raja of Porbandar was caught stealing from the treasury, he blamed his actions on Laxmidas for giving him bad advice. Laxmidas lost his job, the higher income it provided, and any chance for promotion in the future. Hoping to regain the dignity he had lost and to broaden his future opportunities, Laxmidas wanted Gandhi to take advantage of a casual friendship he had made while in England, with the British agent at Porbandar, Sir Edward Charles Ollivant. Gandhi was reluctant to abuse the friendship and thought that if his brother was innocent, he should be able to defend himself. Laxmidas told Gandhi that in the local courts, it was all about influence and did not understand why Gandhi hesitated to defend him. Not having the heart to deny his brother, Gandhi went to Ollivant on his brother's behalf.

Gandhi's acquaintanceship had no bearing in the case. Ollivant accused Gandhi of exploiting their social contact and Laxmidas of conspiracy, saying, "Your brother is an intriguer. I want to hear nothing more from you."[2] When Gandhi continued to defend his brother, he was told to leave and to advise Laxmidas to appeal his case via proper channels. Gandhi quickly realized that meeting the officer in England and seeing him in an official capacity were two different instances and that he would be compromising his own dignity to plead his brother's case any further, if he was truly guilty. Yet family ties were strong and Gandhi plodded ahead, trying to explain to the officer that his brother was innocent.

Gandhi's persistence angered the British officer, and he ordered Gandhi off the premises immediately. When Gandhi did not obey and kept on with his story, the officer called for a servant to have Gandhi removed from his office. Only when the servant appeared and physically removed Gandhi from the man's office did Gandhi realize how insignificant he was to a powerful British representative—in Gandhi's own country. The entire incident infuriated Gandhi and sparked a measure of desire to see reforms in India.

LEARNING TO TOLERATE ANGER

Unable to endure the insult he suffered at the hands of Ollivant, Gandhi wrote a note to the political agent. "You have assaulted me through your peon," he wrote. "If you make no amends, I shall have to proceed against you."[3] Ollivant responded with a note of his own, stating that Gandhi was the one who had been rude. Gandhi had refused to leave, even though he had been asked, allowing Ollivant no other option than to remove Gandhi. Ollivant reminded Gandhi that he had not been hurt and dared him to proceed with his claim. Gandhi was devastated. Not only had he been humiliated, as he saw it, but he had not made a bit of progress in his brother's case. In fact, knowing the officer's distaste for his brother, he had probably only made matters worse.

Sir Pherozeshah Meta happened to be in Rajkot at the same time, but Gandhi was too embarrassed to see him. Instead, he sent the case against the British officer to Mehta through a clerk and begged for his advice. Mehta set him aright. He told Gandhi to expect such treatment, as most clerks and barristers were treated similarly, and that if he wanted his business to thrive in India, he would forget the entire misfortune and stop being immature. The advice, of course, shocked Gandhi, but he took it and swallowed the insult. He determined never to attempt to rely on friendship in a business situation again, regardless of the circumstance. The incident provoked an epiphany; Gandhi realized that he was the underdog in his own land.

Gandhi's estimation of Kathiawar politics continued to break down as he witnessed one petty slight against Indians after another. Indians had to kowtow not only to British representatives but also the representatives' assistants, and he soon realized that to rise in his profession as a barrister, he would have to become involved in the underbelly of Kathiawaren politics. The idea was horribly distasteful to Gandhi, who had always found it hard to tell lies, because politicians are renowned for their prevarications.

The redemption from this moral dilemma came in an offer from South Africa, which was received by his brother, in March 1893. Dada Abdullah & Company, formerly of Porbandar, was involved in a huge lawsuit against another South African merchant, and the case had dragged on for a long time. Although the company had engaged barristers and clerks already, they were particularly interested in Gandhi's counsel, as he had attended school in England. Their letter persuaded Laxmidas to show Gandhi how the venture would not only be good for his career, but also allow him to see another part of the world. Soon after, Gandhi discussed the possibilities with one of the firm's partners in India, who assured Gandhi that Dada Abdullah & Company was in need of his English expertise and that all his expenses would be paid. The company even offered a first-class fare both ways.

Gandhi did not hesitate to accept the offer, even though he would be gone from home for another year. He realized that a salary, net of his own living expenses while in South Africa, would help the family. Plus, he was ready to see more of the world. England had only whetted his appetite for travel and adventure, but he was reluctant to leave his family again.

On October 28, 1892, Gandhi and Kasturba had had another son, whom they named Manilal. As a father of two, leaving his family again was even more complicated for Gandhi than when he had gone to England, but after some discussion, both parents decided that the separation was only for a year and that Gandhi needed the experience to further his career.

An agent of Dada Abdullah met Gandhi in Bombay in April 1893 and told him that there were no first-class berths available on the ship; however, Gandhi managed to secure himself a berth with the captain, who liked the young Gandhi. They played chess together, although Gandhi was a novice and had much to learn. The captain tried to teach him more about the game, but Gandhi lost interest once he left the ship and never played chess again. The friendship changed somewhat when they took port at Zanzibar and the captain invited Gandhi and an English friend to go ashore with him. Gandhi had no idea where the captain intended to take them, and he was completely aghast when the trio ended up at a brothel. Gandhi just stood quietly by the doorway in shame and rebuked himself for having entered the room at all, and as he left, he thanked the Almighty for having saved him from what he saw as a grievous sin.

HOSTILITY IN SOUTH AFRICA

Toward the end of May 1893, Gandhi reached Durban in the British Crown Colony of Natal (now Kwazulu-Natal), a small province on the east coast of South Africa. An Indian wearing a British suit was unusual, but still an Indian, and Gandhi recognized the discriminatory atmosphere in Durban immediately. Dada Abdullah himself, who had written to Gandhi's brother with the offer of employment, met Gandhi at the harbor. Gandhi immediately noticed that although he was a prominent businessman, the British snubbed him. Abdullah seemed to be used to such treatment, whereas Gandhi found it abhorrent.

Even more upsetting was that Abdullah perceived Gandhi as someone requiring a level of upper-class attention and expense, and had no idea what kind of work he was to give the young barrister. The case for which Gandhi had been summoned was taking place in the Transvaal, a province that historically existed to the northwest of Natal.[4] Abdullah would not send Gandhi to try the case because he had not proven himself, and so Gandhi was stuck in Natal until further notice.

However, Gandhi's time in Natal was not wasted. Abdullah proved to be an astute man, even though he was uneducated and had learned only rudimentary English. His knowledge of the language was sufficient for day-to-day operation of the company, but he needed someone who could speak and write well for the finer elements, such as contracts and other legal issues. At that time, Abdullah held the largest Indian firm in South Africa and he was a Muslim. He was proud of his heritage and happy to discuss religion with Gandhi, who thereby acquired a practical knowledge of Islam.

Gandhi's first personal brush with adversity in Durban came when he accompanied Abdullah to court, where the magistrate asked Gandhi to remove his turban. Rather than comply, Gandhi left the courtroom. He could not understand why Muslims were permitted to keep their turbans on, whereas other Indians were asked to take them off. But little that he had seen pertaining to Indians in South Africa was fair.

The Indian population in that country had been classified: There was the class of Muslim merchants who referred to themselves as Arabs; another class comprised Hindu clerical workers; and there were the Parsis, who were also clerical workers and called themselves Persians. These classes interacted both professionally and socially. But the largest class of Indians living in South Africa comprised Tamil and Telugu, from the southeast of India, and North Indian indentured and free laborers. Many of these came from the Dalit caste.

Beginning around 1860, after the abolition of slavery in the British Empire in 1834, manual laborers were in high demand to work the Natal sugar plantations, where native Zulus refused to work. Poor Indians, hearing that they could earn money and buy land of their own, as opposed to suffering a life of continual poverty in India, signed contracts to labor in South Africa for three years on a salary of ten shillings a month with free room and board. When the indentured agreements ended, they were given an option of extending their contracts another two years. After the prolonged period, the indentured servants were permitted to remain in South Africa as free men or to return to India as they wished. Most decided to stay, because the opportunity in South Africa far outweighed that in India. Women joined their men and colonies sprang up; their population was substantial by the time Gandhi hit South Africa's shore.

Indentured workers were known by other Indians as *girmitiyas* or *girmit*, both bastardized forms of the English word *agreement*, but the English called them *sammis*, taken from the *swami* ending of many Tamil last names, or *coolies*, meaning porters. *Sammi* was more contemptuous, but the term *coolie* was so widespread that the indentured laborers came to refer to themselves that way. Usually, laborers only interacted with higher-class Indians or whites in business matters.

Among Europeans living in South Africa, Indians were seen as being unclean, although the urban Indians, such as Gandhi and other professionals living in Natal, saw themselves as highly civilized. Still, Gandhi was known as a "coolie barrister" in South Africa, and he knew that continuing to wear his turban would only bring trouble. If he was forced to remove his hat, he would be swallowing an insult. This was not something Gandhi could stomach, so he changed his hat to a western style and avoided any confrontations.

However, Dada Abdullah chastened him for doing so and said that it would have a bad effect on his people. Abdullah argued that Gandhi's capitulation would compromise all those who wished to wear turbans and that an English hat made him look like a waiter. No self-respecting Indian ever wanted to be a waiter, as they saw the profession as degrading. This sparked Gandhi to action. He wrote a letter to the press, describing the incident at court and defended his right to wear a turban. The matter was broadly argued among the people—pro and con, English and Indian—for some time. Subsequently, Gandhi wore his turban nearly all the while he remained in South Africa.

After only his first week in Durban, Gandhi had gathered Dada Abdullah's confidence and was sent to settle the company's case in Pretoria, the Transvaal. He set off by train with first-class accommodations; however, when the train stopped in the Natal capital of Maritzburg that evening, the conductor asked Gandhi whether he would need bedding for the night. Gandhi declined, saying he had brought it with him, and there was no further event. But about 80 kilometers north of Durban, at Pietermaritzburg, another passenger spotted Gandhi and looked him over with contempt. He seemed disturbed to see a "colored" man in first class, and Gandhi's suspicions were proven when the passenger came back with two train officials, who told Gandhi that he had to transfer to a third-class compartment. Gandhi was aghast. He told the official that he was holding a first-class ticket, but the train master told Gandhi that was not an issue. The official insisted that Gandhi move immediately or that he would call a constable. Gandhi refused to leave his car, and a police officer came and threw him and his baggage off the train. The train left the station without him.

MAKING DECISIONS

Sitting in the freezing train station, Gandhi was too upset to ask for his overcoat, which was still in his luggage, under the railway authority's charge. Shivering, he assessed his situation, wavering between going back to India and staying in South Africa to fight for his rights. Ultimately, he determined that it would be cowardly to run away and not meet his obligation to Dada Abdullah, so he decided to take the next train to Pretoria and to suffer the insults flung at him, if need be. The following morning, Gandhi wired the general manager of the railroad, and also informed his employer of the incident. Abdullah met with the station manager in Durban, who upheld his employee's actions, saying they were justified. The following day, Gandhi's first-class berth in the next train was reserved and he rode to Charlestown without further incident.

Because no railway was available between Charlestown and Johannesburg, the next leg of Gandhi's journey would be via stagecoach, for which Abdullah had already booked passage. Yet when the station manager saw that Gandhi was Indian, the manager cancelled his ticket. The ticket would have allowed Gandhi to ride inside the coach, but Indian passengers were never permitted to ride with white travelers, only to ride in seats on the outer sides of coaches. Gandhi feared losing, another day during the journey, so he quietly took the insult and rode outside the coach, next to the driver, as the secondary driver had offered Gandhi his seat.

This accommodation would not last. When they arrived at Pardekoph, the man who had been kind to Gandhi told Gandhi to ride sitting on the footboard on a dirty piece of burlap, and said, "Sammi, you sit on this. I want to sit next to the driver."[5] Being called *sammi* and the implication of sitting at the man's feet was more than Gandhi could bear. He refused to sit on the footboard and demanded he be placed inside the coach. With that, the coachman boxed Gandhi's ears, grabbed his arm, and yanked him from the seat, but Gandhi clung to a brass railing on the side of the coach. The assailant continued to swear and scream at Gandhi while tugging furiously, but Gandhi would not let go. The scene made the passengers aboard the coach plead for Gandhi's release. They offered to allow him to sit inside, but Gandhi's persecutor backed off and allowed Gandhi to keep his seat next to the driver. Although Gandhi's immediate problem was solved, his assailant continued to threaten him with violence throughout the rest of the trip. Gandhi was happy to see friendly Indian faces waiting for him when they arrived at Standerton.

Gandhi wasted no time in informing the stagecoach company of the raw treatment he had received at the hands of their employee. He demanded an assurance that he would be treated as the other passengers on the next leg of the journey and be permitted to ride inside the coach. Even though no apology was offered, the stationmaster did reply that the men Gandhi rode with would not be with him on the next run. He was guaranteed a seat inside the coach and subsequently rode to Johannesburg without further trouble.

When Gandhi arrived safely that night, he recognized no one at the station to meet him and took a cab to the Grand National Hotel to secure lodging for the night. When he asked for a room, the hotel manager told him that the hotel was full and dismissed him brusquely. Gandhi then asked the cab driver to take him to the shop of a friend, where he found the man Abdullah sent him to meet, Abdul Gani. Gandhi told Gani about his lodging problems, and Gani had a good laugh over Gandhi's naïveté. "Only we can live in a land like this," he said, "because, for making money, we do not mind pocketing insults, and here we are."[6] And he proceeded to explain the Indian place in South Africa to Gandhi, which was at the bottom of the pecking order, aside from Africans, who were seen as even lower than Indians. Africans also lived under British rule and, like Indians in India, were treated like underlings in their own land.[7]

Gani also informed Gandhi that he would have no choice but to travel third class to Pretoria, as things were less advanced in the Transvaal when compared with Natal. First- or second-class accommodations were not even available to Indian passengers there, but Gandhi would not accept the situation. He wrote a note to the stationmaster and explained that he was a barrister, that he always traveled first class, and that he would expect a first-class ticket to be waiting for him when he arrived at the station. Rather than wait for a response, Gandhi walked to the station in his best suit and asked for the ticket at the ticket window. The stationmaster asked whether he had sent the note, and Gandhi assured him that he had. The stationmaster told Gandhi that he would give him the ticket only if he would promise to make no fuss if the conductor insisted that he move to third class and if Gandhi would promise not to mention where he had acquired the ticket. Gandhi reluctantly agreed to the man's stipulations and purchased the ticket.

Gandhi told Gani what had happened and Gani was astonished. Gani worried that Gandhi would have difficulty on his way to Pretoria just by being himself and not acquiescing to such well-established issues, and his fears were well founded. When the train conductor came to examine the passengers' tickets and saw Gandhi sitting in first class, he angrily signaled for Gandhi to move to third class by pointing. Gandhi refused, saying that he had a first-class ticket, which he readily produced. The conductor told Gandhi that it did not matter and that he expected him to move. The only other passenger in the car, an Englishman, rebuked the conductor. "Don't you see he has a first-class ticket?" he asked. "I do not mind in the least his traveling with me."[8] Then the Englishman turned to Gandhi and told him to make himself comfortable where he was. The conductor snapped back, "If you want to travel with a coolie, what do I care?" and left the car.[9] Without further incident, Gandhi reached Pretoria that evening.

MORE INSULTS

Once off the train, Gandhi worried that he would not be able to find a place to stay and was reluctant to enter into further confrontations. Luckily, an African American gentleman, standing near Gandhi at the train station, heard him inquiring about accommodations to the stationmaster, who was not being remotely helpful. The African American told Gandhi that he could take him to an American hotel where he would be accepted. Gandhi worried slightly about taking the stranger up on his offer, but he was exhausted and wanted a place to stay.

When the pair arrived at Johnson's Family Hotel, the African American man spoke to Mr. Johnson. Johnson agreed to give Gandhi a room, but only on the condition that he ate his meals in his room. Johnson told Gandhi that he was not prejudiced, but his white guests might be offended and even leave the hotel if he permitted Gandhi to eat in the dining room with them. Gandhi acquiesced to the man's wishes and said that he would make other arrangements the following day. However, an amazing scenario unfolded. Johnson appeared at Gandhi's door shortly thereafter and confessed his guilt over treating him prejudicially. He said he had spoken to his other guests, who had no compunctions about Gandhi sharing a dinner table with them and that he should stay at the hotel as long as he liked.

The following day, Gandhi went to see A. W. Baker, as his employer had instructed. Baker received him warmly but said that he had no work for a barrister, as they had already engaged strong counsel. He said that he would use Gandhi to gather research. Baker also apologized that he had not found suitable accommodations for Gandhi yet, but took him to see a poor widow, who needed the income from Gandhi boarding at her house. The widow accepted Gandhi as a boarder, and he moved in shortly thereafter.

Gandhi could finally settle down in Pretoria and found himself most interested in Baker's religious background—Christian—which Gandhi wanted to explore further. But Gandhi quickly decided that legal work and religious study were not all he would be about in South Africa. He was angry—angry over the treatment he had received and angry because he knew that every other Indian was swallowing insults, just to survive. He decided not to stand idly by and watch this happen any longer. The true Gandhi was poised to emerge.

NOTES

1. Quoted in Gandhi, *An Autobiography*, p. 87.
2. Quoted in Wolpert, *Gandhi's Passions: The Life and Legacy of Mahatma Gandhi*, p. 31.
3. Quoted in Gandhi, *An Autobiography* p. 98.
4. The region now forms all or part of the provinces of Gauteng, North West, Limpopo, and Mpumalanga.
5. Quoted in Gandhi, *An Autobiography*, p. 113.
6. Quoted in Gandhi, *An Autobiography*, p. 115.
7. Gandhi's future demonstrations for equality were only those for Indians to be equal to whites, without regard to native Africans. He saw himself as part of the white tribes, not part of the black society.
8. Quoted in Gandhi, *An Autobiography*, p. 117.
9. Quoted in Gandhi, *An Autobiography*, p. 117.

Chapter 4

AWAKENING A DIMINUTIVE GIANT

The humiliations that Gandhi had suffered since his arrival in South Africa rankled him. Knowing his fellow countrymen were receiving the same treatment or worse only added to his indignation, and he decided to study the issue. He first met with Sheth Tyeb Haji Kan Muhammad, who was as influential in Pretoria as Dada Abdullah was in Natal. Gandhi told Muhammad that he intended to contact every Indian in Pretoria because he wanted to learn more about the conditions under which they were living and asked for his help. Muhammad readily agreed.

Pretoria was a good environment to begin this evaluation, as the conditions there were often much worse than those of Natal. Gandhi wrote, "It would be no exaggeration to say that the citizens of Johannesburg do not walk but seem as if they ran. No one has the leisure to look at any one else, and every one is apparently engrossed in thinking how to amass the maximum wealth in the minimum of time!"[1] Gandhi's countrymen in the Transvaal seemed to care not at all for the slights they suffered, seeing the indignities as a cost of doing business.

Gandhi wanted to address those most prominent in the business community and present them with the idea that they were representative of all Indians living in South Africa, and that their behaviors might be a direct influence on the way their brethren were treated. Gandhi asked to meet with the merchants in order for them to share their own experiences with him at the home of Sheth Haji Muhammad Haji Joosab, and primarily Muslims attended the meeting, although a few Hindus were present. During this conference, Gandhi gave his first public speech, concerning business ethics, and informed them of their rights. He expressed his view that honesty in business was highly important; however, his audience expressed a different view. They agreed that to conduct profitable business, a measure of misrepresentation was necessary and reminded him that business and religion were independent. Gandhi responded by showing them how integrity in business could raise their level of esteem with their white clients, who expected them to be dishonest. He also told them that he had noticed a lack of hygiene among the merchants and that cleaning up would also promote esteem. He reminded them that although they had disparate religions, they were all Indians and projected an image of their country. He also suggested that they form an association to intercede with authorities on the Indian community's behalf and offered his time and energy in seeing the organization to fruition.

Comments from the audience made Gandhi realize that he had made an impression but also that the men struggled to get their ideas across to him and to each other, due to their dissimilar Indian languages and dialects. He encouraged the audience to learn English. Not only would the language help them to communicate with each other, but to strengthen their position in the community because they would be able to speak directly to the English people, rather than in broken terms or through an interpreter. Gandhi offered to teach English to anyone who desired to learn. The gathering ended with an agreement to meet on a regular basis.

These conferences helped Gandhi to know the Indian people living in Pretoria, the Transvaal. Many of them were formerly of the Orange Free State, west of the Transvaal, where Indian merchants had already been driven out by discrimination and high taxes. Gandhi learned that only Indians who labored at menial jobs, such as waiters in hotels, remained in the Orange Free State, and the idea worried him that Indians could be slowly driven out of South Africa completely. Even in the Transvaal, only Indians who paid a poll tax of £3 could enter; they were not permitted to own land, except in ghetto areas set aside for them; and they were not even permitted to walk on footpaths, which were reserved for the whites. Indians also had to abide a curfew; however, those who passed as Arabs were exempt from the law. Gandhi himself had to carry a permit to be allowed in the streets after 9 P.M. and was once pushed from a footpath and kicked into the street by a police patrolman.

Not only this policy, but others pertaining to transportation, lodging, and simply being alive, had made South Africa a hostile environment for any self-respecting Indian. Gandhi set out to improve the state of affairs of Indians in all of South Africa, although changing the state of affairs in the Transvaal would be difficult. Indians were not citizens of the country. The Transvaal was not of the British Empire; therefore, Gandhi's people were already considered aliens. Being Indian just made matters worse. Yet, Gandhi could not devote all his time to the betterment of conditions for his fellow countrymen; he still had a case to settle for Dada Abdullah and Company.

BECOMING A BARRISTER

Gandhi began to prepare the case for his employer immediately, which kept him in Pretoria for one year. Although he could not make much impact on improvement of conditions there, he spent the time studying the Indians' plight. He also took time to increase his education in spirituality and attained experience in his profession, which gave him the confidence he needed to succeed as a lawyer.

One important lesson Gandhi garnered from his legal experience furthered his lifelong quest for truth and gave him great insight into the law. He realized that when only truth was employed, the law naturally came to its side. During this time, Gandhi also saw that the function of a lawyer was to unite people at odds. As many contemporary law practitioners know, settling a dispute is usually better than having it drag out in the courts. Gandhi grasped this idea while in South Africa and later came to have the reputation of mediator. His cases rarely went to court.

While pursuing his spiritual training, Gandhi attended the Wellington Convention, organized by Protestant Christians. Gandhi's friend, A. W. Baker, hoped that the convention would induce Gandhi to become a Christian. However, the trip was not as pleasant as Gandhi had hoped because he continued to find racial prejudice along the way. Gandhi's traveling companions would not tour on Sunday, the Christian Sabbath, and the companions were forced to stay in a station hotel along the way, over night. Only after much persuasion was Gandhi permitted a room at the inn, without dining room privileges. Because he did not want to embarrass his traveling companions, he yielded to the slight and ate his meal in his room.

Once at the convention, Gandhi was inundated with the Christian religion but had difficulty in believing that Jesus was the only incarnate Son of God and that anyone who believed in Jesus would have everlasting life. He also disagreed that the sins of the world had been forgiven through Jesus's suffering and death. He saw the passion of Christ merely as a metaphor for sacrifice and thought that, in those terms, Hindus had far surpassed Christians in terms of suffering. He came away from the convention without faith that Christianity was the greatest or the only religion; however, he was not convinced that Hinduism was the perfect religion, either: If Untouchables could be part of the Hindu religion, it was deficient in regard for human rights.

Persistent uncertainty set Gandhi on a new binge of spiritual reading. He met Edward Maitland, coauthor with Anna Kingsford of *The Perfect Way*. He also read *The New Interpretation of the Bible* and, most importantly, Tolstoy's *The Kingdom of God Is Within You*. Tolstoy's work overwhelmed Gandhi through its promotion of fundamental truth, independent thinking, and exemplary morality. "[Tolstoy's] starting point was Christ's precept of 'Resist no evil'... the very text which had stirred Gandhi. In his view it implied a total renunciation of force."[2] Gandhi would begin a correspondence with Tolstoy that would last until the author's death in 1910. Around the same time, Gandhi also wrote to Indian religious thinker Shrimad Rajchandra, who would come to be Gandhi's philosophical mentor.

A NEW CAUSE IN DURBAN

Back in Pretoria, Gandhi achieved a compromise in the legal suit for his client Dada Abdullah & Company and no longer had reason to stay in the Transvaal. Gandhi made plans to return to Durban, where Dada Abdullah had planned a party for him in anticipation of Gandhi's return to India. Before the party began that evening, Gandhi perused the Durban newspapers. He spied a small item regarding a new bill then before the legislature, known as the "Indian Franchise," which would deprive Indians of their right to vote. The proposal infuriated Gandhi. To him, it was a way of denying one of the few rights Indians had and he was concerned that it was a first step in squeezing Indians out of Natal altogether, as he had seen done in the Orange Free State. Yet, when Gandhi presented Dada Abdullah and the other merchants at the party with the issue, the men shrugged it off. Abdullah told Gandhi that the only time they had even cared to vote was to keep one of their local politicians in office. Otherwise, the right was not important to them; it could remain or be denied, and it would not disturb them. They saw no controversy.

Gandhi's fury quickly infected the men present. They asked Gandhi to remain in South Africa an extra month, if the young barrister thought the issue was so important. Abdullah volunteered himself and the other businessmen as acolytes, if Gandhi would only direct them. At this suggestion, the other partygoers declared their assent by begging Gandhi to remain and offering to pay him. Yet, Gandhi informed the men that payment was out of the question. Public work should be for the good of the community, without recompense. If he were to assume the onus of leading them, he agreed only to accept donations for necessary office expenses. Everyone readily agreed, and Gandhi found himself assuming the role of leader.

Another meeting to discuss the Indian Franchise law was soon held at the home of Dada Abdullah. In attendance was the most influential man in Natal, Sheth Haji Muhammad Haji Dada, and with him were other rich and powerful Indians, such as Sheth Abdulla Haji Adam. Also in attendance were Natal-born Indians, who lived somewhat apart from those native to India. Overall, the native South Africans of Indian descent were better educated and overwhelmingly Christian. Although they were treated similarly, they were viewed by Indian immigrants as part of the British community. Gandhi brought all factions together by inviting the Durban Court Interpreter and the Headmaster of a mission school there to translate. With a common cause, differences in religion, language, and geographical allegiances were forgotten.

The group knew that time was short for them to form a plan of action, as the Indian Franchise bill had already gone to a second reading in the legislature. Gandhi fueled this urgency by suggesting that the legislators' pro arguments had been strengthened up to that point by Indian apathy, which only helped their adversaries to prove that Indians were not entitled to the vote. Immediately, the committee drafted a plea and wired it to the Speaker of the Assembly, to inform him of the new anti-bill alliance and to request that further discussions of the bill be postponed in the legislature, until the Indians had time to devise a formal complaint. Five hundred Indian signatures were on copies of their plea, which were delivered to the House of Legislature, the press, and to Sir John Robinson, the Premier of Natal. Because they produced written evidence of substantial support from the Indian community, an extension of two days was granted by the Speaker of the House.

Gandhi drew a formal petition for presentation to the Legislative Assembly that night and five copies were handwritten out. Each was taken by one of the merchants to obtain as many signatures as possible. They were not to accept signatures, however, if the signatories did not fully understand what they were affirming. After achieving as many signatures as possible, the petition was sent to the Legislature, and read, "[Your petitioners] earnestly beseech your Honourable Assembly to reconsider your decision; or to appoint a Commission to enquire into the question as to whether the Indians residents in the Colony are fit to exercise the privilege of franchise, before proceeding further with the Bill."[3] *The Times of India,* which also received a copy of the petition, came out in endorsement for Indian demands, which further enthused the community.

This initial success, although an important step forward, glued Gandhi to Natal. He could not leave in the midst of a battle, although following his vow of fidelity to his wife. He pined for her and his children. Kasturba was sorry that her husband was not coming home as he had promised; however, she was relieved that he had found success in his profession. In total, they had only been together four years of their eleven-year marriage; she was used to separations, but she worried for her sons. As Gandhi had been away so much of their young lives, they did not really know their father.

In deference to his position and with the intention of bringing his wife and children to live with him in South Africa, Gandhi thought that he should set up a proper household in a good location. Though he would not accept public funds for his support, he did get the community to agree to provide £300 in legal work for him to complete each year. The community argued with him and said they should at least provide for his living expenses, since he was not drawing a salary to help them, but Gandhi was adamant and reiterated that work done for the good of the community should not be remunerated. Twenty merchants agreed to provide him with the necessary work to fund his personal support.

Gandhi then applied for admission to the Supreme Court of Natal as an advocate; however, the Legal Society of Natal found the idea to be repulsive. They claimed their reasoning had nothing to do with race, but with the fact that Europeans were in the minority in South Africa. If too many "colored" people were admitted to the bar, whites would be overwhelmed and have no protection under the law. A prominent lawyer was hired to fight Gandhi's application, but in the end, the court ruled that color had nothing to do with the law. Gandhi had fulfilled the requirements of his admission and was told to stand and take the oath of admittance; however, the judge insisted that he remove his turban. Gandhi, realizing his limitations in that situation, did so immediately.

Gandhi's friends had become more militant with enthusiasm for the Indian agenda and some, even Sheth Abdullah, thought Gandhi had betrayed them by removing his head covering. Gandhi reasoned with them, saying it was a custom of the court that no hats of any kind were to be worn in the Supreme Court and that he had only complied with those customs. He had come to truly appreciate the beauty of compromise, a policy that would come to play in his philosophy of nonviolence in later years.

GANDHI, THE POLITICIAN

When the Franchise Bill passed, Gandhi was not daunted and planned to follow through with sustained agitation. He wanted Lord Ripon, the

Colonial Secretary in London, to veto the bill and saw constant pressure as the only means of attaining his cooperation. To achieve this goal, the Indians decided to create a viable political organization to run their campaigns. Gandhi recommended the body be termed the Natal Indian Congress, and on August 22, 1894, the organization began to take shape. Annual dues were set at £3 a month, with wealthier members paying a higher fee at their own discretion, to subsidize members who could not afford the entire amount. Gandhi insisted that no operations be undertaken unless sufficient funds were available to pursue them, and because of his prescience, the Natal Indian Congress never went into debt. As the organization's first executive secretary, he continued to insist on strict rules of accounting so that every debit and credit involving the organization was recorded, precluding any charges of financial misappropriation.

Congress meetings were held once a month or more often, if required. A substantial membership sprang up, and it was important to Gandhi that all views be heard. As few members were accustomed to public speaking, Gandhi taught them the rules of procedure and stressed the need for brevity. Before long, the audience became fully involved in every discussion, giving rise to side benefits from the myriad ideas that were presented. The Colonial-Born Indian Educational Association was founded under the auspices of the Natal Indian Congress by the educated class of Natal-born youths, which allowed them to debate issues of primary concern to their special community, and in conjunction with this organization, a small library was founded. The Natal Indian Congress also became an information outlet with the aim of familiarizing people in England and India with conditions in South Africa.

Gandhi wrote two pamphlets for this purpose. In the first, "An Appeal to Every Briton in South Africa," he wrote in regard to the Indian Franchise law, "To say that the Indian does not understand the franchise is to ignore the whole history of India. Representation, in the truest sense of the term, the Indian has understood and appreciated from the earliest ages. That principle—the *Panchayat*—guides all the actions of an Indian. He considers himself a member of the *Panchayat*, which really is the whole body civic to which he belongs for the time being."[4] The second work was titled "The Indian Franchise—an Appeal." This also pled for support in blocking the Franchise measure. Both pamphlets were widely distributed and earned some sentiment from the European class, and in fact, Lord Ripon did refuse the bill as it was originally presented, explaining that no element of the Empire could discriminate based on color.

But for all its benefits, the Natal Indian Congress was not perfect. Although the membership included Indians from the educated, uneducated, merchant, clerical, and working classes, it still was not a viable organization for indentured laborers because the dues were too steep for them to afford. Gandhi thought that the only way to include them was to provide service to them in some way. The event soon presented itself.

A Tamil man named Balasundaram presented himself to Gandhi, wearing raggedy clothes. His hat was in his hand, his front tooth was missing, and his mouth was bleeding. He had been beaten by his master, a well-known European from Durban. Gandhi took Balasundaram to a physician directly and asked for written proof as to how the man's injuries were inflicted. He then took the man to the local magistrate to press the case. A summons was issued against Balasundaram's employer. Yet, this was not Gandhi's intention. He wanted Balasundaram released from servitude, as there was a possibility for further injury by his employer, especially after involving the law. No indentured man could voluntarily leave service without prosecution or imprisonment for breaking his contract. Only the Protector of Indentured Laborers was able to cancel contracts or transfer laborers to other masters, so Gandhi contacted Balasundaram's employer and threatened to proceed legally unless he agreed to transfer his injured servant to another proprietor. The man readily agreed to avoid prosecution. Gandhi found alternate arrangements for Balasundaram and, through this, became the hero of indentured servants throughout the region. He had given them hope.

AN UNFAIR TAX

Gandhi helped those who had come to South Africa under indenture again in 1894, when the Natal Government proposed a £25 per head annual tax on each freed servant. Those who had completed their three or five years of service and had gone into farming and business for themselves had outshone the European businessmen in key areas. The Indians were better farmers because they were able to grow more crops on each parcel of land, making the local varieties sell for lower prices. They had also introduced Indian vegetables and mangoes, which became popular. Some of the formerly indentured Indian businessmen had done so well that they were able to buy large tracts of land and build bigger houses, and the Europeans did not like the competition.

They were also uneasy with Indian culture. Gandhi wrote, "The Europeans throughout South Africa had been agitating against Indians on the ground of their ways of life. They always argued that the Indians were very dirty and close-fisted. They lived in the same place where they traded. Their houses were mere shanties. They would not spend money even on their own comforts. How could cleanly open-handed Europeans with their multifarious wants compete in trade with such parsimonious and dirty people?"[5]

Combined with their extreme differences in religion, racial hatred grew and ultimately found its outlet in the £25 tax. However, this was in lieu of other stringent measures, such as returning the Indians to India before their indentures expired. Since the Indian government would never have acceded to this quietly, the £25 tax was a way to keep indentures poor and out of business.

Gandhi and his cohorts stepped in to vigorously oppose the tax. As the average indentured Indian made only £168 per year, the proposed tax could devastate a family, as it applied to any adult, any female child over the age of 13 years, and any male child over the age of 16 years. A hypothetical family of four with older children would have to pay £100 per year or nearly 60 percent of their yearly income in taxes.

It is not clear whether the Natal Indian Congress had any impact on the situation, but the Indian Viceroy at that time would not approve the £25 tax, though he did agree to a reduced £3 levy. Yet, even at £3 per year, the tax was still a great hardship on the indentures.

A JOURNEY HOME

By 1896, Gandhi had been in South Africa three years and was anxious to return to India for six months. He wanted to spread the word about conditions in South Africa, and as it appeared that his work there would stretch into several more years, he made a decision to bring his wife and children back to South Africa with him. On June 5, he boarded the *S.S. Pongola*, bound for Calcutta, and during the voyage, took up the study of other Indian languages. He knew that a basic understanding of them would surely come in handy in South Africa, so he began to read books on Tamil so he could communicate with people from the Madras region and Urdu in order to get closer to the Muslims.

Gandhi landed in Calcutta on July 4, 1896 and the same day, boarded a train bound for Bombay; however, at Allahabad, he visited a pharmacy, causing him to miss the train. As he realized that he had come to be publicly noticed because of his work with the Natal National Congress, he decided to stay in Calcutta for a while, working toward educating Indians about the plight of their brothers and sisters in South Africa. *The Pioneer*, which was published in Allahabad, had come to the attention of Gandhi because of its anti-Indian rights policy. Gandhi asked for and got an appointment with Mr. M. Chesney, the editor.

Chesney told Gandhi that he was sympathetic to the problems shared by Indians in South Africa and India, and that he would provide space in his paper for anything Gandhi wrote, as a counterpoint. Chesney could not agree to support any Indian demands, due to the editorial viewpoint of the paper, and explained to Gandhi how he had to allow the colonial viewpoint equal weight. The arrangement suited Gandhi because his purpose was to inform Indians and Europeans alike regarding the conditions in South Africa, and as the newspaper's readership was mainly colonials, publication of the information in *The Pioneer* would satisfy at least one aim.

After this initial success, Gandhi rushed home to Rajkot. He received a warm welcome from his family, and Kasturba went about preparing all of Gandhi's favorite meals. However, the couple had very little time together, as Gandhi was busy working the whole time he was at home.

A first task was to write a pamphlet outlining the Indian condition in South Africa. Gandhi published his work on August 14, titled "The Grievances of the British Indians in South Africa: An Appeal to the Indian Public." It had a green cover and came to be known popularly as "The Green Pamphlet." Gandhi kept nothing back concerning the mistreatment Indians had received in South Africa, writing:

> The man in the street hates him, curses him, spits upon him, and often pushes him off the foot-path. The Press cannot find a sufficiently strong word in the best English dictionary to damn him with. Here are a few samples. "The real canker that is eating into the very vitals of the community", "these parasites", "wily, wretched semi-barbarous Asiatics", "A thing black and lean and a long way from clean, which they call the accursed Hindoo", "He is chock-full of vice and he lives upon rice. I heartily cuss the Hindoo", "Squalid coolies with truthless tongues and artful ways".... The vagrant law is needlessly oppressive and often puts respectable Indians in a very awkward position.[6]

Ten thousand copies of "The Green Pamphlet" were printed and sent to every newspaper and important leader in India. Gandhi enlisted the help of his children in the project, as well as other schoolchildren in the neighborhood, and the work was completed in only a few days. For their reward, the children received foreign stamps from Gandhi's international correspondence, and he instructed them to begin stamp collections.

The Pioneer was the first to editorialize its summary of Gandhi's work, and the synopsis was picked up by Reuter's news organization and sent off to London. This summary of *The Pioneer* article was further summarized when it was sent on to Durban, and the distorted version claimed that Gandhi had written that Indians in Natal were routinely "robbed, assaulted, and treated like beasts," and that they had no recompense.[7] This distortion of what he had written appeared in the *Natal Mercury* and would have dire ramifications in the future.

FIGHTING THE BLACK MENACE

Soon, plague broke out in Bombay, and the populace of Rajkot panicked. Gandhi quickly joined the Sanitary Visitors' Committee and, along with other members of the group, inspected every home in the city. Ironically, the poor were much more cooperative. They allowed inspections and followed the committees' recommendations, whereas the rich were not only recalcitrant, but Gandhi noted that the sanitation was far worse in their homes than it was in the homes of the lower-class people. Their latrines were untended and housed worms, and the odor was overpowering. Although the committee offered them instructions for sanitation, the strategies were rarely carried out. Church officials were more compliant than the wealthy, but Gandhi found conditions similar to theirs inside places of worship and was highly offended that such unsanitary behavior would exist in houses of God.

Yet, even more surprising to Gandhi were the conditions in the living quarters of the Untouchables. Hindus thought this lowest caste to be the most odious of people, and only one person from the committee offered to go into their living area with Gandhi. What the pair found was astonishing. Not only were Dalit living spaces tidy and clean, but they had no latrines inside their houses and performed bodily functions outdoors, away from where they lived. Gandhi was pleased to see that there would hardly be an outbreak of the plague in the ghetto.

With his plague inspection duties completed, Gandhi went back to notifying others about conditions in South Africa. He had not yet come to see that India was an even worse effrontery to the native Indian, as Indians were nearly as mistreated in their home country. Gandhi still believed that it was beneficial for India to be under the wing of the British government and considered himself a good British subject.

Soon after Queen Victoria's Diamond Jubilee, which marked her sixtieth year as ruler of the British Empire, Gandhi went to Bombay, where he met with Pherozeshah Mehta and Dinshaw Wacha. Wacha was the right-hand man of Mehta and a renowned statistician. When Gandhi provided information regarding conditions in South Africa to the esteemed pair,

Mehta offered his help in organizing a public meeting. They finalized the details, and Gandhi left the group elated by the promise of support for his South African friends.

When he visited his sister Raliatben's home, he found her husband critically ill. As Raliatben was not up to nursing her husband alone, Gandhi offered to take them back to Rajkot, and they readily agreed to the journey. Gandhi tended his brother-in-law day and night, until he died.

LEARNING TO RALLY THE CROWD

Grief could not keep Gandhi in Rajkot. The following day, he found it necessary to rush back to Bombay and attend the meeting set up by Pherozeshah Mehta. He arrived at Mehta's office on the eve of the event and Mehta asked him if he had prepared his speech. Due to his brother-in-law's illness, Gandhi had to admit that he had prepared nothing and that he intended to speak off the cuff. Mehta was adamant that if Gandhi's speech was to be reported in the press properly, it should be structured, written out, and printed before the next morning.

Gandhi followed Mehta's advice, even though he was exhausted. When he saw the crowd waiting for him to speak, he saw the wisdom in Mehta's counsel. As the speech had been prepared so recently, Gandhi opted to read it from the paper. When he began to speak, he trembled, his knees shook, and he could only produce a reedy sound. The huge hall required a booming voice to carry the speech to the audience, which refused to listen. Finally, Wacha stood up and read the speech for Gandhi. At his words, the audience became perfectly still, only disturbing the quiet periodically to applaud or gasp at news of the atrocious treatment of the Indians were receiving in South Africa. This pleased Gandhi, but Mehta's approval of the speech thrilled him more, because it helped him to win many influential sympathizers, including Sergeant Keshavrao Deshpande and Small Cases court judge C.M. Cursejti. Although the two men promised to come to South Africa to help him, none ever did. Only one man was openly hostile to Gandhi's attempts at reforms in South Africa and told him it was frivolous to return, that he was wasting his time. The man's words did not upset Gandhi, as the man also said that Gandhi's efforts were needed at home and that India suffered to lose him. The man only stiffened Gandhi's resolve to return to South Africa which he saw as his patriotic duty. Countries are not determined by geographical regions alone, but by the people who inhabit them, Gandhi reasoned.

Mehta smoothed Gandhi's path to other influential men of India, as well. After leaving Bombay, Gandhi went to Poona, where he met B.G. Tilak, a leader of the radical wing of India's nationalist movement, and Gopalkrishna Gokhale, an Indian nationalist leader, who would soon become Gandhi's political mentor. Both men welcomed Gandhi warmly and became his allies. They helped to arrange another meeting of influential Indians in Poona, and Gandhi came away from the event feeling even stronger.

The support continued in Madras, where Gandhi found wild enthusiasm for his cause. During the Madras meeting, his speech was also warmly received and "Green Pamphlets" were in short supply, as the people were eager to read further. Sergeant G. Parameshvaran Pillay, the editor of the *Madras Standard,* provided columnar space for Gandhi to express his views on the situation in South Africa and encouraged him to contribute regularly.

Calcutta, however, provided Gandhi's first negative response. He visited the "Idol of Bengal," Surendranath Banerji, one of the founders of the Indian National Congress, which had been established in 1885. Banerji told Gandhi that he thought the people would be apathetic to troubles in South Africa. Banerji thought that the ills of India far outweighed the importance of problems in South Africa. Without Banerji's support, there was no meeting in Calcutta. Two newspaper editors there were not only unreceptive but treated Gandhi rudely and told him that there was no end to visitors such as him, pushing causes for the wrong reasons. However, editors of *The Statesman* and *The Englishman* newspapers obtained long interviews from Gandhi, which were both published in full. Gandhi remained friends with Mr. Saunders of *The Englishman* for many years.

With these interviews in circulation, Gandhi was on the verge of obtaining the meeting he sought in Calcutta, but a cable arrived from Durban. Parliament was about to reopen for the season and Gandhi's presence was required. The message asked him to return to South Africa as soon as possible. He was afforded free passage for himself and his family aboard the steamship *Courland.* On November 30, 1896, Gandhi, Kasturba, their two sons, and the son of Gandhi's sister set sail for Durban. The total passengers onboard equaled about 800, of which about half were en route to the Transvaal. Gandhi had no idea that danger awaited him when he reached the shores of Africa.

NOTES

1. Mohandas K. Gandhi, *Satyagraha in South Africa* (Ahmedabad, Gujarat, India: Navajivan Publishing House, 1928), p. 12, http://www.mahatma.org.in/books/showbook.jsp?id=3&book=bg0023&link=bg&lang=en&cat=books.

2. Ashe, *Gandhi*, p. 65.

3. Mohandas K. Gandhi, "The Honourable The Speaker and Members of the Legislative Assembly of the Colony of Natal the Petition of the Indians Resident in the Colony of Natal," June 28, 1894, *Collected Works of Mahatma Gandhi Online*, Vol. 1, pp. 147–48, http://www.gandhiserve.org/cwmg/VOL001.PDF.

4. Gandhi, "The Indian Franchise," December 16, 1895, *Collected Works of Mahatma Gandhi Online*, Vol. 1, p. 287.

5. Gandhi, *Satyagraha in South Africa*, p. 36.

6. Gandhi, "The Grievances of the British Indians in South Africa: An Appeal to the Indian Public," August 14, 1896, *The Collected Works of Mahatma Gandhi Online*, Vol. 1, p. 360.

7. Quoted in Arun and Sunanda Gandhi, *The Forgotten Woman*, p. 70.

Chapter 5

A CATALYST FOR CHANGE

When Gandhi boarded the steamship *Courland* with his family, the steamship *Naderi* also set sail. Dada Abdullah & Company owned both ships, which carried free and indentured passengers to Durban and points west, mainly the Transvaal. By this time, Gandhi had already decided on a mode of dress for the family, in order to make them seem more sophisticated than mere residents of backwater Rajkot. As the Parsis were regarded as the most sophisticated of Indians among the Europeans in Natal, Gandhi adopted a Parsi style of dress for his wife and children. Kasturba wore the longer Parsi sari with a long-sleeved blouse, and his sons wore coats and trousers. All wore shoes and socks, which were unnatural for the boys and their mother, as they had customarily been barefooted or in sandals. The whole family often complained of sore feet.

Not only the new dress mode was ill-suited to the Gandhi family. They were used to the emotional comfort of Rajkot—the food, the companionship, the behaviors they had known since birth. Kasturba was particularly unhappy with eating at a table, using utensils rather than fingers, and keeping her mouth shut while eating to avoid the slurping noises she had customarily made all her life. Moreover, boiled vegetables and bread were not particularly filling or satisfying to her or the children. The Gandhis were anxious to get to their new home, where Kasturba would be able to cook the foods they enjoyed.

However, their arrival would not be as soon as they had hoped. Only four days from their destination, a violent storm arose, and colossal waves tossed both ships about violently. December is a summer month in the southern hemisphere, so monsoons are always a hazard at that time of year; but the storm of 1896 was particularly dangerous, and the passengers were terrified. Although they were Muslims, Hindus, Jews, and Christians, among other religions, they prayed together for the storm to subside. Many passengers became ill from the constant rocking and rolling, including Kasturba and her sons. Gandhi was the only passenger who did not succumb to the sickness. It was a long 24 hours of misery, but the sea finally calmed and many prayers of thanks were offered. The ships finally made it to the African coast on December 18, and Kasturba vowed never to set foot aboard a sailing ship again.

Both the *Courland* and the *Naderi* arrived at Durban the same day, but neither ship was permitted to enter the harbor. Anti-Indian sentiment was brewing in South Africa, as shown in the comments of Sir Godfrey Lagden, the Commissioner of Native Affairs in the Transvaal at that time. He remarked, "The lower castes who form the mass [of the Indian immigrants] are as a rule filthy in habit and a menace to the public health."[1] He was a staunch proponent of segregation.

Strengthening the increasing paranoia among Europeans in Natal, news of the plague in India had traveled to Durban. As a prudent precaution, the citizens insisted that medical examinations be required of all immigrant passengers before the ships were permitted to release their human cargo. Should either of the ships have shown any evidence of infection or illness, quarantines would ensue for both ships, even if only one passenger on one ship was ailing. Both ships were required to sail yellow flags, to indicate they were under quarantine, at least until the examinations were complete. Although a doctor found no indication of illness aboard the *Courland*, he ordered a 5-day quarantine because signs of the plague took 23 days at the outside to develop, and they had only been at sea for 18 days. However, there was more behind the quarantine than medical safety.

Just the notion of plague had caused panic in Durban. The Europeans held daily meetings, and it was suggested that they collect the money to pay Dada Abdullah & Company to send their ships back to India, rather than risk bringing the plague to Natal; however, Dada Abdullah was adamant about allowing the ships' passengers to land and would not listen to other options. Meanwhile, passengers on both ships became frantic over rumored threats of being thrown into the sea should they not return to India.

Gandhi believed that he was the real target of these problems, due to his publication of "The Green Pamphlet." Partly to assuage his guilt and partly because the captain asked him to do so, he undertook the role of peacekeeper among the passengers. He assured them that everything would be worked out and told them not to worry. He also sent calming written messages to the people aboard the *Naderi* to help allay their fears. He organized games and dinners aboard the *Courland* while they waited for the conflict to end.

MORTAL DANGER

Meanwhile, the charges against Gandhi were blowing out of all proportion. On shore, there was talk that Gandhi had gone to India specifically to stir trouble in South Africa. He was also accused of lading the ships with passengers in hopes of bringing more Indians to Natal in order to drive the whites out. Both statements were untrue.

On January 13, 1897, after 19 days at sea and 25 in quarantine, the ships were permitted into the harbor and Indian passengers were able to safely go ashore, except Gandhi and his family. Word had reached the ship's captain that because of the European outrage over what they perceived Gandhi had done, his life was in danger. Harry Escombe, the Attorney General of Natal, sent word through the captain to advise Gandhi to leave the ship after dark, when Escombe would escort the Gandhis to their home. However, this plan would not be carried out.

F. A. Laughton, the Dada Abdullah & Company's agent and legal advisor, went to the captain and asked to take Gandhi away from the ship immediately. He told the captain to ignore Escombe's plan and went to speak with Gandhi himself. Laughton told Gandhi that by leaving the ship like a thief in the night, he was giving credence to the rumors surrounding him, and that if Gandhi was not afraid, he should allow his family to drive to the house of Jivanji Rustomji, a trusted member of the Natal Indian Congress and a wealthy Parsi businessman. He lived about two miles from the port. Laughton and Gandhi would follow the family's carriage on foot to show the crowd Gandhi had nothing to hide. This plan suited Gandhi's dignity better, and he quickly accepted Laughton's advice.

Immediately on disembarking, Gandhi was recognized and the crowd repeatedly shouted his name. This brought the attention of others, and soon an entire crowd surrounded Gandhi and Laughton. Fearing the worst, Laughton hailed a rickshaw, although the mob frightened the driver away. Then Laughton and Gandhi were surrounded by the crowd and separated, and the crowd unleashed a hail of stones, bricks, and rotten eggs at Gandhi. His turban was snatched away and the crowd kicked and punched him, until he was bruised and bleeding. To catch his breath, Gandhi grabbed onto a porch railing, while the crowd continued to pull at him and assault him.

Gandhi's rescue came via the police superintendent's wife, Mrs. R.C. Alexander, who opened her umbrella and stood between Gandhi and the crowd. A young Indian man saw the melee and ran to the police station to inform Constable Alexander of the disturbance. Immediately, Alexander took a force of policemen to the scene, which surrounded Gandhi and led him to meet his family, who had already arrived safely at their destination.

Inside Rustomji's house, all seemed peaceful and quiet, but outside a mob surrounded the house. While trying to cajole the crowd into dispersing with no success, the constable sent a message to Gandhi to tell him that if he wanted to preserve himself, his family, and his friend's property, he would be wise to quickly leave the place in disguise. Gandhi was torn. He had done nothing wrong and rued the idea of sneaking away. Yet, he concluded that leaving was the only way to protect the people he loved and the property of Rustomji. He donned a police uniform and tied a scarf over a plate placed atop his head to serve as a helmet. Two detectives, also in costume, led Gandhi through the crowd to a carriage that awaited them at the end of the street and headed for the police station. The ploy succeeded. When the crowd learned of Gandhi's escape, the mob dispersed. Writing in his autobiography 30 years later, Gandhi still wondered whether he had done the right thing.

FORGIVENESS BRINGS PRESTIGE

On hearing the news of the attack on Gandhi in London, Joseph Chamberlain, Secretary of State for the Colonies at that time, sent a wire asking the Natal government to prosecute Gandhi's attackers. But Gandhi refused to proceed legally. He did not blame the people for believing the Reuter's report and told Attorney General Escombe that the people would regret their actions when the truth came out. He also blamed Escombe for not righting the wrong before things got out of hand. Escombe asked Gandhi to put his denial for action into writing so that he could present it to Chamberlain and thanked Gandhi for allowing the situation to quell.

With the intention of clearing Gandhi's reputation, a reporter from the *Natal Advertiser* requested an interview. During the meeting, Gandhi not only refuted the charges verbally but was able to provide the reporter with written copies of the speeches he had made in India, along with "The Green Pamphlet" and his other writings. He also made it clear that he had no hand in bringing the Indian passengers aboard the Dada Abdullah & Company ships. The article that appeared in the *Advertiser* struck the Natal population profoundly, as it proved Gandhi's innocence and castigated the mob, and owing to his decision not to press charges, his prestige among the entire community of Natal increased.

Gandhi wanted his family be accepted by Natal society. He spent time getting them settled in their new two-story, five-bedroom home on the palisades, which had a large balcony over a veranda, overlooking the port. The property entrance was through an iron gate, which opened into a small garden, leading to the front door. The carpeted living room held a sofa, a round library table, two lounge chairs, and a bookcase with books than had been collected by Gandhi, including biographies of Indian leaders and volumes on religious topics, which had been his cornerstones of religious training.

Gandhi soon considered religious and general education of the children in his household. His nephew was 10 years old at the time, and his sons were 9 and 5, but there were no Indian schools in which to enroll them. They might have attended European schools in Natal, but they would only have been admitted because Gandhi was their father. No other Indian children were permitted to attend those schools. Aside from eschewing preferential treatment, he worried that the children would be subject to ridicule by their white classmates and ruled out sending them to European institutions. Christian mission schools were also available, but Gandhi preferred to teach his family in Gujarati, rather than English, as the mission schools would have required. Gandhi opted to advertise for a British teacher, whose teaching would be supplemented by Gandhi's own lessons. He found an acceptable governess for £7 a month, but the arrangement did not last.

Gandhi intended to teach the boys himself, but the lessons only took place when he was able to give them, which was sometimes late at night or very early in the morning, when the children were least receptive. Gandhi struggled with sending the children back to India to be properly educated and eventually sent his son and his nephew to India boarding schools for a few months. But he had to bring them back to South Africa. His eldest son, Harilal, never forgave Gandhi for not giving him the same educational advantages that Gandhi had had himself, and he left to attend high school in Ahmedabad as soon as he was able. The other children received education from Gandhi sporadically over time, but none ever graduated from formal schooling.

As with his sons, the new life in South Africa was disquieting for Kasturba. There were no traditional prayer places in the new home and the kitchen was uncomfortable for her. She was used to cooking while squatting next to the small coal-burning traditional stove, and Gandhi had to give her instructions on using the six-burner stove. Kasturba also lamented the need to prepare meals alone, while standing, rather than participate in cooking as a communal activity shared by the women of the house in India. For the first time in her life, she found preparing food and cooking to be drudgery and was very lonely for her former life. Rather than fall into a vortex of misery, she took interest in all that was going on in Gandhi's world and soon became his helpmate in serving the community. Yet, a time soon came when the couple was at odds.

HARSH DEMANDS

In late 1897, Kasturba learned that she was pregnant, and Gandhi's strict ideals and her Hindu upbringing came into conflict. Each member of the Gandhi household was expected to empty and clean his or her own chamber pots each morning, and Gandhi expected Kasturba to help him with any that had been neglected. Kasturba's pregnancy had become difficult and she did not feel up to such an unappealing task. She was not only disgusted, but angered by his demands and even shamed. She had been raised to believe that such work was reserved for the Untouchables, and she resented his decree that she must defile herself in such a manner.

Gandhi watched Kasturba carrying and emptying the chamber pot of a guest one morning, while weeping at her feelings of such disgrace. He said to her, "I will not stand this nonsense in my house."[2] Then, he took her by the hand and dragged her to the front gate, readying to push her into the street. Kasturba sobbed and said, "Have you no sense of shame? Where am I to go?"[3] Her words shamed Gandhi, who brought her back inside the gate. His vivid remembrance of the episode in his autobiography, written 30 years later, obviously caused him remorse. He could be most compassionate when it came to strangers, but his own wife had often been the recipient of his impatience over the family's inability to adhere his own principles immediately, without question. This incident, more than any other, changed the way Gandhi related to Kasturba for the rest of his life.

Gandhi's compassion for his family and his fellow humans continued to grow, and he soon took up nursing in a small charitable hospital. He dispensed medicines, emptied bedpans, and did what other menial duties were required of him. He spent two hours at the hospital each morning, performing menial tasks, and he relished the peaceful feelings that the work gave him. Gandhi's experiences at the hospital were also useful to his family. Two of his sons, Ramdas and Devadas, were born while the Gandhis lived in South Africa, and Gandhi prepared himself for each delivery, in case a doctor or nurse was unable to come to their aid.

His third son was delivered by a nurse, but Gandhi's prenatal education was of inestimable worth when he had to deliver his fourth son, Devadas, himself.

About this same time, Gandhi began to contemplate the value of physical love and came to believe that controlling lust was high in spiritual value. He seriously considered taking the vow of *brahmacharya*, which includes celibacy and prescribed meditations with influence from Shrimad Rajchandra, his spiritual advisor. Gandhi had always been of the opinion that sex was part of the solemn vow of marriage and that only the act of procreation made sex necessary. Gandhi had always been faithful to his wife, although the occasion to be disloyal had presented itself more than once, but even sexual relations with his spouse gave him reason for guilt. He began to feel that sex was no longer necessary, as he had four thriving children, and wanted no more. He believed in controlling population growth, to allow future generations to derive the full benefit of life on earth.

Gandhi considered the vow of *brahmacharya* seriously after the birth of Devadas. Rajchandra, who was also married, showed Gandhi that the devotion of servants to masters was more estimable than that of wives to husbands. Affection is a normal part of the marriage bond, yet servants have no implied union with their masters; no love binds them, unless servants assume that devotion of their own free well. This idea haunted Gandhi, until he came to realize that by having sex with his wife, without the need to produce offspring, he would inadvertently cause her to be the instrument of his lust, and as long as he continued in this pattern, his fidelity to her meant little. He could take the vow of *brahmacharya*, only if he disregarded his carnal lust and did so through self-control. Gandhi and Kasturba began to sleep in separate beds, and to avoid his desire, he only lay down at the very end of the day when he was completely exhausted. Although he had initial lapses, he had taken first steps toward achieving his final goal.

IMPERVIOUS TO RIDICULE

Along with this quest for self-control, Gandhi was already involved in a quest for a simpler life. He realized that his laundry bills were quite high, and along with that, it irked him that the laundryman was slow in getting his clothes back to him. He had to keep more than two dozen shirts and collars, which were separate items of clothing at that time, to sustain his daily requirements while waiting for his laundry to return. Gandhi decided to do his own wash. Not having any idea how to perform the process efficiently, he bought books on the subject and made Kasturba study with him. Rather than a chore, Gandhi looked on his laundry experiences as a pleasure.

Gandhi's first self-washed and ironed collar had too much starch and he had been afraid to iron it well, as irons at that time were not electric. One had to place an iron on a hot stove to heat it sufficiently to press clothes, and flatirons had no mechanism with which to regulate temperature. Clothes were easily scorched if one was not experienced and careful. Therefore, when Gandhi wore the collar, not only was it wrinkled, but flakes of starch fell from it throughout the day. Gandhi explained to his barrister colleagues, who were having a laugh at the sight of him, that it was his first attempt at washing and ironing. They snickered and asked whether laundries were scarce. Not one to be upset by teasing, Gandhi told them that doing laundry was enjoyable and that he would continue to wash and iron his own clothes.

Of course, Gandhi's friends did not understand why. Neither could they understand when he dared to become his own barber. When a British barber in Pretoria had adamantly refused to cut Gandhi's "black" hair, referring not to the color of his hair but to his skin, Gandhi bought his own barber scissors and cut his hair with a mirror. He had terrible trouble in cutting the back, and when his fellow lawyers saw the mess he had made of himself, he was once again ridiculed. Gandhi explained that he had been refused by the barber, and the laughter stopped. No one blamed the barber for having snubbed Gandhi. They realized that had the barber deigned to cut Gandhi's hair, he would have lost his other customers.

Around this same time, Gandhi became involved in a war for riches—the South African or Boer War. The cape of Africa was originally settled by the Dutch East India Company. Yet, by the end of the eighteenth century, it was mainly occupied by the British, who ultimately took control of the territory during the French Revolutionary and Napoleonic Wars. Unhappy with what the Dutch settlers saw as biased administration by the English, some made their "Great Trek" north, to parts just beyond the Orange River, in 1838. These Boers (from the Dutch language, meaning farmers), fought with the Zulus and the English, and near midcentury both the Orange Free State and the Transvaal fell under Boer control. Their independence was formally recognized in the 1852 Sand River Convention and, in 1854, by the Bloemfontein Convention. Yet, the relationship between the British and the Boers began to unravel when diamonds were discovered in 1869 at Kimberley, situated in the territory of Griqualand West. Control over this region was disputed between the British and the Orange Free State, but they avoided conflict when Britain bought out the Orange Free State's claim for £90,000.

A federation of states within southern Africa was promoted by Lord Carnavon in the mid-1870s; however, the Boers were wary. They saw the federation as an attempt to bring their territories back under British control and resisted the idea, although in 1877, the British easily annexed the Transvaal, as the region was near complete bankruptcy. The initial relationship was one of suzerainty, whereby the suzerain—in this case the Transvaal—retains independent leadership, while remaining under the protection of its sovereign, the British Empire. However, the preliminary agreement was renegotiated in 1884 at the London Convention, allowing the Boers and their leader, Paul Krueger, to deny that any suzerain relationship existed when the British tried to pursue it in later years. Further disputes arose when gold was discovered in the Transvaal in 1886, leading to bitter struggles for control of the area and, eventually, to war.

When the Boers declared war in October 1899, Gandhi's sympathies lay with the Boers, as he identified with the people wanting to rule the land they had made their own and with the Boer women and children who had been concentrated in British-run camps, under harsh conditions. He still felt allegiance to England, however, and thought that if he expected the rights of a British citizen, that it was his duty to participate as a member of the British Empire, saying, "Our existence in South Africa is only in our capacity as British subjects. We have been proud of our British citizenship ... and what little rights we still retain, we retain because we are British subjects. It would be unbecoming to our dignity as a nation to look on with folded hands at a time when ruin stared the British in the face."[4]

IN THE LINE OF FIRE

Gandhi did not condone the violence and inhumanity of war, but he wanted to contribute by establishing an ambulance corps to transport injured men from the battlefield. He was not daunted by British officials who refused his services, as they believed that Indians were cowardly and would not take the risks the job would require. Gandhi went ahead and pursued training for his men via Dr. Booth from the charitable hospital where he had been working and also obtained certificates of physical fitness for all of the men involved. Still, when the Indian corps asked the government to use their training in the front battle lines, they were told that they were not needed.

Never one to settle for an answer he did not like, Gandhi went through another channel—the Bishop of Natal, who welcomed Gandhi's plan readily and agreed to help Gandhi secure the dangerous assignment for the Indian volunteers. When the Boers became stronger than the British had anticipated, the army finally came to welcome the Indians' offer, and the ambulance corps of approximately 1,100 men, comprising 300 free and some 800 indentured Indians, went off to provide medical assistance for the British troops.

Each day the corps marched within the line of fire, carrying the wounded on stretchers a distance of 20–25 miles. Though their bravery and service was remarkable, the team was disbanded in only six weeks, as their services were no longer needed. The war had not ended, but the British decided to slow the battle and wait for fresh recruits from England. Even this short stint as an ambulance service further enhanced the prestige of the Indians among the Europeans, and the newspapers all published laudatory articles regarding their heroism. About 40 corps leaders received the War Medal, and their relations within the Natal community were greatly improved.

To continue this goodwill, Gandhi aimed to improve the conditions of the Indian community from within, as well. Europeans constantly charged that Indians were sloppy and dirty, and even Gandhi had to admit that this was often true. The headmen had begun to be more aware of their personal habits, but Gandhi thought it was time for a full house-to-house inspection when reports of the plague in Durban sprang up. He had the approval of city officials for this, but he was still met with insults or polite rebuff by those who thought that personal hygiene and tidiness were too much work. Yet, overall, Gandhi's campaign for reeducation of the public was a success.

After Gandhi's duty in the Boer War ended, he decided that it was time for him to take his family and return to India. The people reluctantly gave their assent, but only with the hope that if they needed Gandhi again within one year's time, he would return to Natal. To this, Gandhi agreed and several farewell gatherings were held in his honor. Not only did he receive gifts at each party, but many were expensive gifts of gold, silver, and diamonds. Although this might have pleased others, Gandhi was distressed. He thought he had no right to the gifts, owing to his policy of not being paid for public work and decided to return them. Kasturba, having given up her own jewels to support her husband's education, was not pleased at his decision, but his children easily agreed to the plan. Gandhi and his wife had terrible arguments before Kasturba reluctantly succumbed to her husband's will.

LEARNING POLITICS

By December 14, 1901, Gandhi was back in Rajkot, but on December 17, he was already en route to Bombay. The Indian National Congress was to meet on December 27 in Calcutta, with Dinshaw Wacha as its president, and Gandhi had been invited to attend.[5] He met with Pherozeshah Mehta and Wacha aboard Mehta's private train car on his way to Calcutta from Bombay, but Mehta told Gandhi that not much could be done for him at the conference. He asked how they could consider the problems in South Africa when Indians had no power in their own land. Though Mehta and Wacha agreed to put forth a resolution asking for equality for Indians in South Africa and abolition of the £3 tax, they were quite negative about any bill's effectiveness regarding improvement of conditions in South Africa. However, they were sure the resolution would pass. Gandhi was not satisfied with the lack of enthusiasm for his goals but had to acquiesce to the elder statesmen.

Once the train reached the camp where the Indian National Congress delegates were staying, Gandhi quickly ran into prejudice among his own people and it upset him. The higher-caste delegates thought that contact with Tamils would pollute them, and so the Tamil kitchen was separated by a fence. In fact, it was kitchen, washroom, and dining room in one and filled with smoke so thick that it choked the people inside. Gandhi lamented that the delegates of congress put so much stock in the caste system, and he saw irony in that unsanitary practices were high, even among those of the highest castes. The latrines were so few and so poorly maintained that Gandhi asked for a broom just so he could clean one for his own use. Some delegates did not even bother to use the facility at night, but often relieved themselves out the windows or on the streets. Even though Gandhi might have cleaned up the messes with the help of other volunteers, he could find no one to help him, and as the job was too large for him to undertake on his own, nothing was accomplished. His grandson wrote, "Bapu [Grandfather] believed this was one way to break caste taboos—to emphasize that all honest work was worthy, no essential work was lowly."[6]

In view of this belief and wanting to gain experience in all things congressional, Gandhi volunteered for clerical duty at the Congress and was given the task of answering correspondence. Gandhi was nothing if not humble, and when the Congress Secretary complained that his servant was not available to dress him, Gandhi buttoned his shirt. This meekness paid off as it helped him to know the men and to understand the workings of Congress in only a few days. Gandhi would soon be ready to use it as his instrument.

At the end of that year's congressional session, Gandhi's resolution on South Africa was finally put before the members. He was allowed five minutes to speak for its worthiness, which pleased him immensely. Yet, the members were restless and ready to leave, and because Gokhale had seen it, understood it, and backed it, no one else seemed interested to know more about it. Just before beginning to speak, Gandhi recognized that Gokhale had written a poem to praise foreign emigration and when Gandhi read it, he realized its weight. He read it aloud for the audience and then proceeded to talk, but when a two-minute warning bell sounded, he sat down, thinking that his speaking time had ended. The resolution passed anyway, but Gandhi was not happy that the members had passed it without understanding or caring much about it. However, as a first step, he was still pleased that it passed before the Congress ended.

Gandhi stayed on in Calcutta and visited some of the local gathering places. He ran into Gokhale at one of them and was invited to stay in Gokhale's home. Gandhi accepted but did not show up at once for fear that the invitation had not been sincere. Days later, Gokhale approached Gandhi and rebuked him for being so shy. He said that he intended that Gandhi do congressional work and that he needed to get out and meet people. In politics, reticence would do him no good. From the first day of his month-long stay with Gokhale, Gandhi was introduced to the cream of Calcutta society and came to feel like the elder statesman's younger brother.

To Gandhi, Gokhale never seemed to waste a moment. He spent all his time—public and private—working for the common good, and Gandhi was impressed by his total honesty. Gokhale's main concerns were poverty and oppression, as they were the main concerns of India, and he was adamant about gaining his country's independence.

BECOMING ONE WITH THE PEOPLE

Before returning to Rajkot, Gandhi also felt the need to cleanse and edify his spirit by traveling through India via train as a third-class passenger. In preparation, Gandhi filled a box with food and purchased a long coat and a canvas bag (to hold the coat, when not needed), a clean dhoti, a towel, and a shirt. He also took along a blanket and a jug of water. Gokhale saw him off at the platform and wished him a good journey. Gandhi's final destination would be Rajkot, but he planned to stop at Benares, Agra, Jaipur, and Palanpur along the way. He stayed one day in each place and at religious or charitable inns (*dharmashalas*) each night. His first stop would be at Benares, where he wanted to visit an old acquaintance—Annie Besant, who was ill.

Third-class accommodations were appalling to Gandhi. The compartments were filthy and the travelers were herded like sheep. Yet, he blamed his traveling companions for the condition of the train, as they were apt to throw garbage on the floor, spit tobacco, and smoke. He also objected to their screaming obscenities and other behaviors that occurred without regard to those traveling with them. His solution to the problem had many facets. He wanted educated and civilized people to travel third class, so that they might instruct the regular third-class passengers on points of civility. He also wanted them to plague railway officials with reprisals until such conditions were improved. He told them to stop providing bribes to improve their own conditions and never abide others who broke the rules.

When Gandhi arrived at Benares, he insisted that he wash himself in the Ganges River, not only to keep to sacred ritual, but to cleanse himself of the unsanitary conditions he had endured from Bombay. He first visited the Kashi Vishvanath temple, which he had learned about while practicing law in Bombay. What he saw when he arrived was akin to what Jesus saw when visiting the Hebrew temple in Jerusalem. He had expected a solemn atmosphere, conducive to meditation, but found a noisy bazaar. He was quite disturbed, especially because he could do nothing to change it. He also visited Annie Besant, but only briefly, as a gesture of respect.

Gandhi continued on his trek through India via third-class accommodations and, on February 26, 1902 reached his final destination of Rajkot to begin work as a lawyer. Gandhi had success in cases he pursued in Kathiawar and was soon offered a job in Bombay. With some hesitation, he quickly set out to take it.

NOTES

1. David Arnold, *Gandhi: Profiles in Power* (London: Pearson Education, 2001), p. 47.
2. Quoted in Arun and Sunanda Gandhi, *The Forgotten Woman*, p. 87.
3. Quoted in Arun and Sunanda Gandhi, *The Forgotten Woman*, p. 87.
4. Quoted in Wolpert, *Gandhi's Passions*, p. 46.
5. The Indian National Congress met in a different city in India each year, usually with a new president to lead the meeting.
6. Quoted in Arun and Sunanda Gandhi, *The Forgotten Woman*, p. 70.

Chapter 6

REBOUNDING TO THE TRANSVAAL

Upon the Gandhi family's arrival in Bombay, Gandhi joined the firm of Payne, Gilbert, and Sayani. He was settled in his work and even wrote to Gokhale to offer his services when needed. However, Kasturba and the boys were a bit overwhelmed at the size and population of Bombay, which neared one million people. As a crossroads for commerce, Bombay sported a huge harbor, a cotton factory, and giant railway hubs. Its wide boulevards were lined with palm trees, mansions, and well-manicured landscapes. Bombay was not only an exciting city, it was a wealthy city.

Although Bombay was large and bustling, it was still India and seemed more like home to Kasturba than South Africa had. Her father owned a large textile factory as one branch of his business in Bombay, and her brothers, who had inherited the family business, had homes there, as did many of their other friends and relatives. She did not think of herself as a stranger in a foreign land.

This sense of belonging gave way to feelings of concern shortly after the family moved into their home in the Girgaum district. Manilal, who already been through an attack of smallpox a few years earlier and survived, came down with typhoid, accompanied by pneumonia. The Parsi doctor who came to attend the boy said that he had no medication to cure the illness but encouraged the Gandhis to give their son chicken broth and eggs, hoping the protein would improve his condition. Owing to the Gandhi belief in vegetarianism and that Manilal was only ten years old at the time and could not decide for himself, Gandhi had to make a difficult decision. Choosing not to offer broth and eggs to his son could cost him his life, whereas allowing him to consume the foods was going against Gandhi's personal beliefs and the Hindu religion.

As was typical of Gandhi, he did not waver and told his wife, "It seems to me that God is testing us."[1] Kasturba agreed. There was no guarantee that breaking the regimen of vegetarianism that they believed in so strongly would help his son. Gandhi had read about a remedy that he wanted to try and that he thought would be more beneficial to Manilal. The physician argued that Gandhi was flirting with disaster, but Gandhi proceeded to treat his son himself, with the doctor only looking in to measure the boy's heart rate, the degree of his chest congestion, and his pulse.

The treatment included a course of hydrotherapy, in which Gandhi bathed Manilal in a series of shallow baths, lasting three minutes or less. He also plied the boy with orange juice mixed with water. This process continued for three days even though Manilal's temperature rose to 104 degrees, and Gandhi questioned his decision to treat the boy. Yet, Gandhi continued by wrapping Manilal in wet sheets and covering him with double blankets. Only Manilal's head was visible and Gandhi wrapped it too in a wet towel. The anxiety Gandhi felt over his son's worsening condition forced him to leave Kasturba in charge while he went outside for a walk, during which he prayed for the recovery of his son.

When Gandhi returned home, he found Manilal asking to be released from the sheets and blankets. Gandhi felt his forehead, saw beads of perspiration there, and realized that the fever had broken. He was ecstatic, but the fight was not over. It was 40 more days before Manilal fully recovered. Gandhi was relieved that he had saved his son but also that he had saved his own honor. He delighted in remarking through later years that Manilal was the strongest and healthiest of his sons.

Shortly after Manilal's recovery, Gandhi and Kasturba realized that the house in Girgaum was too damp and drafty, and after the open spaces of Natal, they felt cramped in crowded Bombay. They searched for a new place to live in the northern suburbs of Bombay and settled on a bungalow in Santa Cruz for their new home, which they chose primarily for its sanitary quality. The house was also light and airy and close to the local market and the school that Manilal would attend that fall. They rented the place immediately and quickly felt at home.

RETURNING TO THE FIELD

Just as the Gandhis had settled, a cable arrived from South Africa. The Secretary of State for the Colonies, Joseph Chamberlain, was due to for a return visit, and because of Gandhi's commitment to the people of Natal, he had no choice but to go back. He left his wife and children in Bombay, because he knew he would be away for another year, and Kasturba did not want to disrupt their lives again. Gandhi bought an insurance policy to protect the family in case anything happened to him. He also arranged for Harilal and his nephew to remain at boarding school and moved 23-year-old Chaganlal Gandhi, a close relative, and his family into the Gandhis' Santa Cruz bungalow to act as companions for Kasturba and the children. Chaganlal would also act as Manilal's tutor. Through all the preparations, Gandhi began to realize that the only certainty in life was uncertainty and the only constant was God.

Five young men, who were having difficulty finding their place in India, set sail with Gandhi on November 20, 1902. One of them was 19-year-old Maganlal Gandhi, Chaganlal's brother. Gandhi thought of Maganlal and Chaganlal as "nephews," but they were actually sons of one of his cousins, Khushaldas, with whom Gandhi was very close, as Khushaldas had been raised by Gandhi's parents as their own son. Maganlal and the other young men on the trip were going to help Gandhi with the Natal Indian Congress.

Gandhi was anxious to present another Indian delegation to Chamberlain and started work as soon as he arrived in South Africa. Chamberlain was coming to the continent to promote goodwill with the colonials and to attain a £35 million gift from the colony to England. However, when he met with the Indian group, he disappointed them once again by saying that the Indians' grievances seemed real but that they should try to mollify the Europeans if they wanted to live among them. Although this might have been a devastating blow, Gandhi did not take Chamberlain's comment as a huge setback, as did other Indians. He saw it as realism. Gandhi also knew that Chamberlain had little time and appreciated his forthrightness.

Gandhi was to precede Chamberlain to the Transvaal to meet with him there, as well, but he had no idea how he would enter the territory. After the South African War, the Transvaal was in a state of utter disarray. Even food and clothing were impossible to procure in that region, as all the shops either had closed permanently or had not yet been reopened. Shopkeepers required a permit to get back into the area to replenish their stock, and no refugees were to be permitted back into the area until the shelves were full again. It was a circuitous conundrum, especially for the Indians. Most Indians had difficulty in obtaining a permit to reenter their chosen homeland, but it was not problematic for a person of European heritage.

Retired military officers and soldiers had come into the Transvaal from India and Ceylon, and the onus was on England to support them as residents of South Africa. As the British government felt an urgency to appoint new officers who would oversee the welfare of white British citizens, the retired officers easily took up all posts of authority. A department to see to the needs of the native Africans was quickly created and later a department to oversee the Asiatic population, as well. Indians who wanted to return to or to enter the Transvaal had to apply to the Asiatic Department for a permit, which took several days to process, while their shops were looted and destroyed. And just because an Indian owned a shop in the Transvaal did not automatically allow him or her to receive a permit. Indians needed influence and often had to pay up to £100 even with such advantage.

Gandhi thought it would be impossible for him to acquire a permit on his own, regardless, or perhaps because, of his reputation. He went to see the police commissioner Alexander in Durban, the man who had rescued him from the mob in 1897, and presented his dilemma. He told the commissioner that he had lived in the Transvaal and asked what he could do to get Gandhi back into the territory. The commissioner got him the permit quickly and easily, and Gandhi was on a train in less than an hour.

OUTSMARTING THE RESISTANCE

When Gandhi arrived in Pretoria, the officers of the Asian department were aghast. They had no idea how he had been able to obtain a permit without their knowledge or approval and assumed that Gandhi had entered without one. Department officials prepared to arrest him, but upon learning that he had a permit, their disappointment was evident. Their next step was to foil Gandhi's plan of meeting Secretary Chamberlain, and they quickly asked the leader of the delegation, Sheth Tyeb Haji Khanmahomed, for a list of those involved in the delegation. When they saw Gandhi's name, they asked what business he had in the delegation when he was no longer a resident of the Transvaal. Khanmahomed replied that Gandhi was their representative because he understood their language as well as English. Khanmahomed was quickly dispatched to bring Gandhi before the department officials.

Standing before the department heads with his companions, Gandhi was told that his permit was issued by mistake. He had no home in the Transvaal at that time was told he could not meet with Chamberlain and that he would have to return to Natal. Then, he was dismissed. However, his friends were made to stay and were given a sound dressing down over having invited Gandhi in the first place. Gandhi was used to such treatment and bade Khanmahomed and his group to find another man to lead them. They settled on another Indian barrister, George Godfrey, who ultimately became the spokesman for the group.

But the matter only solidified Gandhi's resolve. Rather than return to Natal, he applied for membership in the Bar of the Transvaal Supreme Court. He did so based on his fear that the Asiatic department would run Indians out of the country, after berating and robbing them. Gandhi decided he could not allow that to happen and set up a legal office in Johannesburg, where 12,000 Indians resided. He expected to be turned down for membership in the high court, and he was surprised to be admitted without trouble. He soon organized the Transvaal British Indian Association, which began gathering evidence against Asiatic Department officials.

Law and social justice were not monopolizing Gandhi's mind while in the Transvaal. As always, spirituality played a big part in his busy life, and he made time to associate with the Theosophists there. He did not join their society in Johannesburg, but he came into close contact with its followers every day, although he did not completely understand them. The main thrust of Theosophy is the cultivation and promotion of brotherhood, but Gandhi thought they were hypocritical as their beliefs and their actions did not coincide. He also thought that they wanted him in their society, not to enrich his spiritual life, but to gain something from him as a Hindu.

Gandhi introduced his Theosophist friends to the *Gita*. For him, it had become a daily reference and he drank from its language as one imbibes daily water. He was most enamored of the words *aparigraha*, meaning nonpossession, and *samabhava*, meaning equality. In studying the meaning of these words, Gandhi realized that he could not follow God unless he gave up everything. Although he might have property, he should act only as its trustee, rather than its owner. He would continue to ponder these ideas while continuing public life.

Over several months, Gandhi had gathered a great deal of evidence against the Asian Department, such as proof that people with no right to reenter the Transvaal, aside from having £100, had been admitted, and that it was still made difficult for Indians who owned businesses there to get back to their homes. Once Gandhi was satisfied that he had enough substantiation to prosecute, he took the material to the police commissioner, who was sympathetic to the problem. He interviewed each witness whom Gandhi presented before him. Although the commissioner was convinced that Gandhi had a sound case, he warned Gandhi that it would be nearly impossible to get a white jury to convict white men in an Indian cause. Gandhi fully intended to put his evidence before the court.

DISAPPOINTMENT AND A NEW VENTURE

Gandhi's operation became intrigue as spies followed him in his daily routines. The Chinese in Transvaal, who were also discriminated against, allied with the Indians in this cause and the overwhelming truth prevailed, but only for two of the officers involved in the case. One of the officers fled but was extradited for trial in South Africa. However, as the police commissioner had predicted, both were found not guilty at the trial and set free. Gandhi was disappointed and revolted by the legal system. Yet, there were two positive aspects of his attempts at righting the wrongs done by the Asiatic Department: First, the bureau cleaned up with the worst officers gone, and second, Gandhi's prestige was further enhanced within the community.

Being Gandhi, he had nothing personal against the officers who were acquitted and even kept silent about their previous misdeeds so they could find alternate employment. Through Gandhi's kindness, he had improved his relationship with the Asiatic Department, as well. He still had disagreements with the department, but overall, these arguments were benign and often helpful to the people involved. Gandhi attributed his actions to an innate sense of *ahimsa,* which means nonviolence. He also believed that *ahimsa* was at the root in his search for truth, which he had always associated with God. To Gandhi, recognizing brotherhood, whereby we are all created equal by the same Supreme Being, was the most important aspect of life. He believed that when one hurts another living thing, the damage reverberates around the world.

Contrary to Gandhi's peaceful beliefs and practices toward others, his own frustration level increased. He had four Indian clerks working for him, but they could not type, so he decided to hire a European clerk. He got the name of a Scottish woman—Miss Dick. Gandhi worried that she might have objections about being employed by a "colored" man, but she had none and began working right away. Before long, Miss Dick became like a member of Gandhi's family. Her work was impeccable and Gandhi entrusted huge sums to her for disbursement and accounting. When it was time for her to marry, Gandhi stood in for her father and gave the bride away. At that point, she became Mrs. Macdonald and quit her job, but she did help when Gandhi desperately needed her.

His next secretary was Miss Sonja Schlesin, a 17-year-old Russian Jew, in whom he came to have complete confidence. When it came time to pay her, she would accept no more than £10 a month, although her skills were worth much more, and argued that she was with Gandhi to learn and to help him because she held his ideals in high esteem. Payment was not an issue. Even Gokhale, who later met the seventeen-year-old Schlesin, considered her to be of high character and thought her to be the best of Gandhi's employees, citing her dedication and courage. Another of Gandhi's European workers was L. W. Ritch, whom he knew as an employee of another firm. Gandhi persuaded the man to come and work for him, and they also formed a strong alliance.

Because of his reputation and his prolific writing for several newspapers by that time, Gandhi was approached by the owner of the first Indian-owned printing press in South Africa regarding the start of an Indian newspaper. The man had already been publishing a newsletter and wanted Gandhi's approval to take the publication to the next level. Gandhi wholeheartedly agreed with the proposal, and the first issue of the newspaper, *The Indian Opinion*, was launched on June 4, 1904.

The Indian Opinion was published weekly in four languages—Gujarati, Hindi, Tamil, and English (although the Tamil and Hindi sections were later abolished)—and Gandhi quickly realized that he would have to contribute funds of his own to keep the paper running. He felt a need to continue publishing the journal, as his reputation was tied up in it, and more importantly, it was the primary source of information for the Indian community. Gandhi thought it was necessary to continue producing the weekly as a point of honor, and he lost nearly all his savings.

Using *The Indian Opinion* to promote his own the ideals to the public, Gandhi's articles appeared in nearly every issue, which taught him the power of the press. When wielded properly, the press is a valuable and needed service, but when abused, the medium can lead not only to misunderstanding but also to disaster. One continuing topic in *The Indian Opinion* had to do with the Untouchables. Gandhi saw them as the providers of the most important social services and abhorred the way Hindus treated them by placing them in ghettos on the fringes of society. He saw himself and the other Indians as the Untouchables of South Africa, and having experienced such treatment firsthand, Gandhi was determined to put an end to such discrimination.

A few months after the paper's first issue was published, Gandhi realized that he had been gone from India longer than the year he had promised Kasturba and, without hope of imminent return, vacillated on sending for his family. He wrote to in a letter to one of his friends, "The question, then, is as to the fulfillment of my promise to Mrs. Gandhi. I told her that either I should return to India at the end of the year or that she should come here by that time. I am most anxious to fulfill that promise. How to do so is the difficulty."[2] Without his wife, Gandhi would be free to pursue civil life, without familial obligations, and at this time in his life, this seemed most desirable. He later wrote to Chaganlal and asked him to persuade Kasturba to remain in India, but he was also aware of his responsibility. Ultimately, he left the decision to Kasturba. He wrote and told her that if she wanted to come to South Africa, she should plan to stay for about 10 years.

When Kasturba got the news, she was not visibly shaken, but inwardly, she was not happy to have to upset her life again. It would mean moving again, away from Chaganlal and his family, with whom she had become very close, and Harilal insisted that he stay in India at his current school. He had been considered a highly intelligent child, so Kasturba was torn. She did not want to leave her son, but neither did she want to spend more time away from her husband. After much consideration, she made the decision to board a ship bound for South Africa with three of her sons, while leaving Harilal behind.

However, Harilal was not on Kasturba's mind when they reached their destination. Ramdas had broken his arm while at sea. The ship's doctor had put it in a sling but said that it must be properly set when the family reached their destination. Rather than take the boy to a doctor, Gandhi again decided to nurse the injury himself. Every day he treated Ramdas's arm with a poultice of mud and fresh bandages, and in a month, the boy's arm was healed.

The family was settled in their new home in Johannesburg by that time, too. Gandhi had rented a large, eight-room house in Kensington, one of Johannesburg's European sections, about five miles from his legal office. Although the furnishings were meager, the home was acceptable and even comfortable for the family.

ENDURING TOLERANCE AND FAMILIAL RESPONSIBILITY

Not all Indians living in Johannesburg were so comfortable. The Indian community was afforded plots of land with 99-year leases, but while the population grew, the land did not increase in size, making the Indian section of the city very crowded. The city provided latrines for the Indian population, which they haphazardly maintained, but neither lights nor roads. The place was completely unsanitary, and the local legislature was approached by the city managers to destroy the locale.

Gandhi knew the sanitation problems in the Indian ghetto were horrific and agreed that the village should be closed to avoid serious disease; however, as a lawyer, he also knew that the Indians had proprietary rights in accordance with the breakage of their leases and were entitled to recompense. Although monetary settlement was offered by the city, Indians had the right to appeal the amount in court and most of the lessees hired Gandhi to represent them. Rather than make money from these cases, Gandhi took only what the court awarded in fees, if the case was won, or £10, regardless of the outcome. He told his clients he would donate half the amount to build a hospital or another important structure for the poor. All of his clients were pleased with his proposal, and of around 70 cases that Gandhi tried, only 1 was lost. His clients had come to call him *bhai* or brother, which seeped into the rest of South African Indian society. He enjoyed the appellation and would continue to be known by the term until he left South Africa.

A REMATCH WITH PLAGUE

Other Indians were not contented, nor were they removed from the ghetto immediately when the city decided to level the village. Owing to the municipal takeover of the land, rather than being proprietors, the Indians were then tenants. The unsanitary conditions worsened, and the Indians living on the land continued to increase in number. As a result, pneumonic plague broke out, and although Gandhi alerted the authorities, he was told that the Town Council of Johannesburg could not assume any financial responsibility.

Pneumonic plague is much worse than bubonic plague because rather than contracting the illness from the bite of a flea, pneumonic plague bacteria are airborne and inhaled into the lungs. The source of the outbreak was one of the gold mines, but the disease was easily passed in the ghetto because of the crowded and unsanitary conditions.

To help with the plague patients, Gandhi enlisted the help of the four young men who had accompanied him from India as they were single and had no families. One of them broke open the lock of a vacant house and Gandhi quarantined all of the plague patients there. The town expressed gratitude for the men's quick action but worried that the building's owner would object to its usage as a hospital for patients with the plague and offered another more permanent site in which to tend patients, but it was miserably dirty and had to be cleaned up before they used it. They also lent a nurse and William Godfrey, a Johannesburg physician, who went immediately to help on hearing the news. Twenty-three patients made it through the first night, yet only two of the patients recovered. The nurse was also infected and died.

Kasturba had offered to help with the sick, but Gandhi told her that she it would be better if she went through the neighborhood and gave information about the disease to the people at risk. Although she was not used to dealing in such a manner with strangers, she realized the importance of the task and went about spreading the news and information about hygiene, spotting plague symptoms, and avoiding contraction of the disease. She had also helped clean the building the city had donated for the makeshift hospital.

The next step was for the city to relocate the Indians living in the ghetto to open-air tents until more suitable accommodations could be made. They intended to burn the village it to the ground after the evacuation. Gandhi thought this was not so much a precaution for the Indian people, but to prevent the plague from spreading among the whites. When news of the city's plans hit the residents of the ghetto, panic ensued. The residents had no bank accounts and usually hid their money or buried it in the ground. Gandhi became their reluctant banker and money literally poured into his office. He spoke with his own banker to set up an account for the funds, but the clerks in the bank were leery of touching the coins for fear they would get the plague. Some £60,000 had to be disinfected before it could be deposited. Gandhi, who always tried to find positive elements in any situation, saw an advantage to the complications in that the Indians learned to invest their money in banks.

A special train transported ghetto residents to a farm near Johannesburg, where the city supplied them with food and other necessities at the city's expense. Many of the Indians were stressed about the uprooting and the lack of proper housing but soon were used to their new lives. Their old living quarters went up in smoke the day after their evacuation, and the plague spread no further.

REASSUMING THE DUTIES OF A FATHER

During the plague outbreak, Albert West, a vegetarian eating companion of Gandhi's, had taken charge of *The Indian Opinion*; Gandhi returned to Natal to discuss its fiscal strength with the press owner, who had given up in disgust. The paper was in turmoil with unpaid debts and mounting losses. He had decided to return to India, and Gandhi took a train to Natal, where the man was staying, hoping to salvage what they had started.

While on the train to Durban, Gandhi read a book he had been given by his friend Henry Polak, a man whom Gandhi had met in the vegetarian restaurant in Johannesburg: John Ruskin's *Unto This Last: Four Essays on the First Principles of Political Economy*. Ruskin wrote, "In fact, it may be discovered that the true veins of wealth are purple—and not in Rock, but in Flesh—perhaps even that the final outcome and consummation of all wealth is in the producing as many as possible full-breathed, bright-eyed, and -hearted human creatures."[3] Gandhi took away three important points from Ruskin's work—that the good of one is contained in the good of all, that all work for pay is equal in importance, and that a life of menial labor is worth living. Gandhi, ready to embrace the principles, later translated the work into Gujarati. Ruskin's work also gave him an epiphany regarding *The Indian Opinion*.

After discussing what he had taken away from *Unto This Last*, Gandhi conferred with West regarding his newly acquired perceptions. He expressed his desire to move the *Indian Opinion* press to a farm, where everyone could share in the work for the same pay, thus cutting expenses and making the newspaper profitable for the first time. West agreed, but not all 10 of the people working at the *Indian Opinion* were ready to move to a remote location. Gandhi and West agreed on a £3 wage for every worker and told the people not ready to move that they could continue to draw their higher salaries while easing themselves into the idea of moving to the farm. The owner of the press was against the idea, saying that Gandhi would destroy all that he had tried to accomplish with the paper.

A PHOENIX RISES

Nevertheless, Gandhi set about finding a farm. He advertised for a plot of land between Durban and the railway station and, within a week, purchased 20 acres about 2.5 miles from the Phoenix railway station and about 14 miles from Durban. The property included a fresh-water spring and some fruit trees. Beside the plot was another 80-acre parcel with even more orange and mango trees and a small cottage. Gandhi completed his real estate deal by buying both lots for £1,000.

Gandhi's old friend Javanji Rustomji, whose home he had used for shelter during the 1886 riot in Durban, came to Gandhi's assistance once again. He supplied workers and building materials to build a shed for the printing press. Although the area was overgrown and infested with mostly poisonous snakes when the workmen began, the 3,750-square-foot structure was ready within one month. After the building was complete, Gandhi enticed others to come and live with him. One was Maganlal Gandhi, who supported Gandhi in all his pursuits, both physical and spiritual. With Maganlal and a few others, publishing of the first issue of *The Indian Opinion* from Phoenix was begun around the end of November 1904. Yet, getting the paper out would be a Herculean task.

Gandhi did not want a motored press, but one that worked with a hand crank, as it was more in line with the agricultural aspect of the farm. Yet, he soon realized that this aim was impractical. Therefore, an oil-fueled engine was installed, and a hand-driven wheel was also installed in case the oil-fueled engine stopped working. The size of the paper was also reduced to make it more practical, as the smaller pages would be easier to publish should the hand crank become their only option. Everyone worked night and day, and because the living quarters were not yet complete, the carpenters slept on the floor of the printing shed at night. But when Gandhi realized that they needed more hands for the paper, he awakened the carpenters and put them to work on the paper, as well, and the first Phoenix issue of *The Indian Opinion* was published on time.

Gandhi wanted to stop working in the legal profession eventually and to earn his daily living by working on the farm and with the newspaper. He also wanted to move his family to the Phoenix Settlement full time. To this end, and to get the community solidified, they constructed corrugated iron houses, but Gandhi was called back to Johannesburg to take care of pressing business while the construction was taking place. As the newspaper and the new settlement depended on his earnings, he had no choice but to return and continue to spend much of his time in the city.

Going back to the simplistic lifestyle Gandhi encouraged at the Phoenix Settlement, things began to change at the Gandhi's Johannesburg home, as well. He lamented the need to keep furniture because of his professional stature—he wanted severe changes at the personal level. They would no longer purchase bread at the bakery, for example, and made their own unleavened bread from whole grains. To grind the grain, Gandhi purchased a hand mill, which took two men to operate. Henry Polak quit his job to join Gandhi at Phoenix and lived in the Gandhi household, along with his wife, Millie. He was often enlisted to help with grinding, but the children helped out as well. Gandhi also hired a servant to help with household duties, but the Gandhi family continued to empty their chamber pots every morning, as Gandhi did not believe it to be servants' work, but a personal responsibility. Gandhi also made it a point to speak in Gujarati to his children for them to learn their native tongue, while Millie Polak taught Kasturba some conversational English. Millie also helped with tutoring Gandhi's sons, as he had less and less time to contribute to their education himself.

Gandhi wanted to change life for others but thought he had failed as a civil servant, and although his law practice was the most successful in Johannesburg at the time, he saw very little of what he had been working toward take root. He wanted to find a way out of the legal system and took decisive action.

FALLING OUT WITH TRADITION

On May 12, Gandhi wrote a letter to his brother Laxmidas, telling him that he would give him all he had saved over time toward repayment of his debt to the family; however, he was taking a personal vow of poverty. He intended to renounce all wealth and stated that he would offer no more in repayment of what the family believed he owed. Although he might continue to earn money, he would keep none of it. Any money or other property that Gandhi might acquire from that time onward would be used to benefit the community. Laxmidas was astounded and deeply hurt. He had run into bad times, and as Gandhi had been successful, Laxmidas depended on his brother to honor the old traditions. He berated Gandhi, saying that he was abandoning the will of his father, that it was Gandhi's place to support the family, as Laxmidas had done in the past. No matter what argument Gandhi presented, Laxmidas would not understand. Gandhi wanted him to realize that by contributing to the community, he was supporting the family in a spiritual sense. Laxmidas only needed to broaden his sense of the word, but the disagreement set a rift between the brothers. Laxmidas stopped communicating with Gandhi almost entirely. Yet, his ire was not piqued over the money. He was ashamed that Gandhi had abandoned his traditional responsibility.

About the time Gandhi began to feel comfortable in Johannesburg once again, it was June 1906, when a Zulu rebellion broke out in Natal over taxation. Zulus, much like Native Americans, had been and continued to be forced out of their tribal lands by a burgeoning European population. To make matters worse for them, the government proposed oppressive poll and hut taxes against them. Although the Africans struggled to keep up by taking servant work in the city, they were overwhelmed by the financial burden and the rebellion began with a single incident. A Zulu chieftain, named Bambata, balked at the taxes, told his tribe to refuse to pay, and when a tax collector showed up, he killed the man. Not wanting to set a precedent, the British sent troops into Zulu territory to quell any potential uprising.

Gandhi had no quarrel with the Zulus and he still thought of himself as a British citizen. He wrote to the governor of Natal to ask about reforming the Indian Ambulance Corps, and the offer was immediately accepted. Gandhi, who had made plans to enlist before even writing the letter, broke up the Johannesburg household and sent his family to live at the Phoenix Settlement. Polak and his wife stayed on in Johannesburg, where Polak would continue his legal studies so that he could assist Gandhi in future legal issues.

But before Gandhi set off for Durban to recruit men for the ambulance corps, he received an upsetting letter from his brother. Without the Gandhis' knowledge, Harilal, who had been betrothed some years earlier, had been married the month before. Gandhi was furious with Laxmidas, who wrote in the letter that he thought it was in the boy's best interest. What Gandhi and Kasturba had not known was that their son had fallen in love after living in close proximity to his intended, and Laxmidas thought them better married than engaging in illicit sex. As Harilal's father, Gandhi saw only Harilal's youth and the fact that he had much to learn before starting a family at issue. The day after receiving the letter, Gandhi wrote to his brother Laxmidas, "Harilal's getting married has no meaning for me."[4] Not another letter would pass between the brothers for years. In fact, their disagreements would continue almost to the time of Laxmidas's death, when he would write to Gandhi and commend his sons to Gandhi's care. Laxmidas also expressed a desire to see his younger brother again but died before this happened.

After repressing his feelings about the situation in deference to duty, Gandhi traveled to Durban. He had already enlisted men from the Transvaal and gathered the rest of his corps in Natal. Of the 24 men who joined him, 4 were from Gujarat, with the balance made up of freed indentured laborers from southern India. Soon after their arrival in Zululand, Gandhi was appointed Sergeant Major. He chose three other men to be made sergeants and one corporal, and the government provided the whole corps with uniforms. On their arrival at the front-line camp, the ambulance corps learned that their main duties would consist of nursing wounded Zulus, as white people would not tend them. They happily took up the chore; however, their work would be punctuated by taunting from the white soldiers, who tried to dissuade them from helping the wounded black men. Gandhi worked to make friends with the offending English soldiers, and they eventually left Gandhi and his men alone. What upset Gandhi more than this discrimination was learning that several of the Zulus' wounds had not been acquired in battle, but via flogging of captured prisoners, which had left festering wounds. Other patients had been friendly to the Zulus and incurred gunshot wounds when they had been mistaken for enemy warriors. Work to bring these people back to health lasted about six weeks.

The horrors of the Zulu Rebellion hit Gandhi much harder than did those of the Boer War. He felt that the skirmishes were less like war and more like manhunts, and to take his mind off what was going on around him, he often lost himself in reflection. He made his final resolution to take the vow of abstinence (*brahmacharya*) upon his return to the Phoenix Settlement.

ABSTINENCE AND *SATYAGRAHA*

The decision to take the vow of celibacy and spiritual denial was not easy to make, although he had another example via an honored friend. Tolstoy had also made the decision to stop serving himself, to serve society, and to become celibate for the balance of his life; however, Tolstoy's decision had affected his wife so vehemently that she became suicidal. Gandhi had backed away from sexual relations with his wife before taking the final vow, but he had not stopped having intercourse completely. Yet, *brahmacharya* would change that. He worried how this decision might upset Kasturba and discussed it with his close associates before approaching her with the finality of the vow he was about to make.

Even Kasturba's grandson does not know how she reacted when Gandhi finally presented her with his ideal. Biographers merely suggest that she accepted it as a good Hindu wife, or even that it was a relief. The first tactic Gandhi used to stay true to the vow was to stop sharing a bed with Kasturba and to stop having private time with her. What ultimately developed was a playful, brother-and-sister type relationship with Kasturba fully accepting her husband's spiritual journey and the poverty he had come to embrace. She did not know that she was about to become embroiled in much more than just Gandhi's ideals. She would soon be enmeshed in a struggle for which Gandhi had been preparing for years.

NOTES

1. Quoted in Arun and Sunanda Gandhi, *The Forgotten Woman*, p. 103.
2. M.K. Gandhi, "Letter to H.V. Vora," June 30, 1903, in *The Collected Works of Mahatma Gandhi*, Vol. 3, (Delhi: Publications Division, Ministry of Inform and Broadcasting, Government of India, 1958) p. 352. http://www.gandhiserve.org/cwmg/VOL003.PDF.
3. John Ruskin, *Unto this Last* (London: J. M. Dent & Sons, 1932), McMasters University, Social Science Department, http://socserv2.socsci.mcmaster.ca/~econ/ugcm/3ll3/ruskin/ruskin.
4. Quoted in Arun and Sunanda Gandhi, *The Forgotten Woman*, p. 137.

Chapter 7

TRUST AND DISAPPOINTMENT

Immediately after taking the vow of *brahmacharya*, Gandhi made radical changes in his lifestyle, but not merely concerning sex. He changed to a diet of fruit and grains exclusively and fasted or had only one meal on holidays. His goal was to learn to consume only what his body needed to survive and to achieve synchronicity with nature.

Kasturba was enduring her own trials at the same time, caused by chronic hemorrhaging. Doctors advised her to have an operation to cure the problem; however, in her emaciated, weakened state, anesthesia could not be administered, and she had to undergo the operation in severe pain. She came through the ordeal well, and the doctor advised Gandhi, who had been called back to Pretoria, that he could travel without worrying about his wife, who would stay behind.

Yet soon after Gandhi arrived in the Transvaal, the doctor contacted him. Kasturba's condition had worsened and the doctor wanted Gandhi to give his permission to feed Kasturba beef broth to strengthen her system. Gandhi left the decision up to Kasturba, although the doctor said he would not consult her in her weakened state. He was adamant that he be given carte blanche in prescribing Kasturba's diet or, he insisted, Gandhi had to return to Durban, where Kasturba was being treated, immediately. Gandhi returned that same day.

The doctor wasted no time in telling Gandhi that he had already given Kasturba the beef broth before he had made the call to ask Gandhi's permission. Gandhi was furious and accused the doctor of fraud. The doctor countered Gandhi's claim by saying that it was within a doctor's realm of authority to prescribe medicine or diet for all patients to save their lives.

As the doctor was a friend, Gandhi quelled his anger but argued that he would never have allowed Kasturba to receive meat or meat products, even if it meant her death, unless Kasturba herself had made the decision to accept that course of treatment. Under those circumstances, the doctor asked Gandhi to remove Kasturba from the clinic, saying that he refused to watch her die.

To settle the dilemma, Gandhi was able to consult Kasturba, who declared that she would not take beef broth or any other sustenance that was counter to her religion, even in her frail condition. She told her husband that she would sooner die in his arms than to pollute her body. Kasturba was placed in a hammock and six men carried her back to the settlement, where Gandhi tended her with hydrotherapeutic treatments. Kasturba slowly grew in strength until she achieved a full recovery.

STRUGGLE WITH THE BLACK ACT

In late August 1906, Gandhi returned to Johannesburg and found a copy of *The Transvaal Government Gazette* of August 22 lying on his desk. In it was the first published copy of the proposed "The Asiatic Registration Amendment Ordinance" (TARA), which came to be known as the "Black Act" or "Black Ordinance," as it seemed to be maliciously pointed at the Indian population living in the Transvaal, and it included stringent regulations. One was that every man, woman, and child had to appear before the Registrar of Asians to apply for a certificate of registration bearing a signature, a full set of fingerprints, and a photograph. The inclusion of women and children in this registration was outside the realm of Indian culture. Indians also raged that the required fingerprinting was akin to treating them like criminals, as criminals were the only people who were fingerprinted at that time. Muslims had additional scruples about their photographs being taken. Those subject to the proposed legislation would also be required to carry their registration cards at all times and to produce them for the police when requested, without warning or reason. Any person who could not produce the registration would be subject to fine or imprisonment. Noncompliance with the registration process, including not showing up before the proposed deadline, meant fine or imprisonment and loss of residence. The law would also apply to minors.

Gandhi not only saw the proposed legislation as oppressive but also feared that compliance with the rule could be the first step in pushing Indians out of the Transvaal. From there, he surmised that the trend would continue until Indians were completely driven out of South Africa. It was not long before government officials were talking about eliminating the "Asiatic cancer" and driving the coolies out within four years' time.[1]

TAKING DECISIVE ACTION

The next day, Gandhi called a meeting in his office, where he heard the outrage of those in attendance. Some offered to die rather than submit if the law passed, and they decided to band together to oppose the initiative. A meeting was called for 2 p.m. on September 11 at the old Empire Theater, where there was standing-room only, with every aisle filled. Gandhi presented his resolutions to the crowd in Hindi and Gujarati, and Tamil and Telgu translators relayed the information for those who were not able to understand the other two languages. Other speakers also delivered impassioned speeches.

News of the resistance spread throughout South Africa, causing Indians to embrace the concept of "passive resistance." Yet, to Gandhi, the united front that Indians had sworn to uphold meant so much more. "Satyagraha is soul force pure and simple," he wrote, "and whenever and to whatever extent there is room for the use of arms or physical force or brute force, there and to that extent is there so much less possibility for soul force."[2] To clarify terms, Gandhi ran a contest in the *Indian Opinion* with a small prize to the person who could best describe these ideals in a new word, and the victor turned out to be his protégé Maganlal Gandhi. He came up with the word *Satagraha*. In Gujarati, *sat* means truth and *agraha* means firmness. Although Maganlal won the prize, Gandhi changed the word to *Satyagraha*, and the word became the buzzword for the struggle against Indian oppression in South Africa and in India. Gandhi biographer Geoffrey Ashe wrote, "Satyagraha was destined to develop into a reasoned system of unarmed action offered not merely as an expedient to use where force was impossible, but as a weapon superior to force."[3]

The Satyagrahis' spirit was only rising when TARA was overwhelmingly passed by the Transvaal Legislative council in October. The Satyagrahis had made some impact on the law because when it finally passed, it no longer required women to be registered. Gandhi realized that before it took effect, the law still had to be approved by the King of England. To prevent this, Gandhi suggested that a delegation be sent to Great Britain to inform the Secretary of State for the Colonies and the Secretary of State for India of the hardship relating to the proposed legislation in hope that the proposed law would be denied or amended. On September 21, Gandhi's plan was accepted by the Satyagrahis. Gandhi and H.O. Ali, one Hindu and one Muslim, were the chosen candidates for the presentation, and they set sail for England on the S.S. *Armadale Castle* on October 1, 1906.

The two men drafted a proposal to present to the English cabinet and had it printed the moment they arrived on British soil. Subsequently, they alerted the Indian National Congress and advised the members of their intent. The Congress gave its approval for the South African delegation to proceed. They also drafted a well-known and respected member of English society and an Anglo-Indian, Sir Lepel Geffen, to introduce the South African delegation to Lord Elgin, the Secretary of State for the Colonies at that time.

Even with proper preparation and protocol, Lord Elgin was not encouraging. Even though he said that he sympathized with the Indian situation in South Africa, he told the delegation that he was dealing with other pressing problems, but he agreed to do what he could for them. The group also met with Lord Morley, the Secretary of State for India, who gave a similar response. Sir William Wedderburn went so far as to call a meeting of the Committee of the House of Commons for Indian Affairs, where the South African delegation also presented their case, and they met with the leader of the Irish party and with the British Committee for the Indian National Congress. The delegation wanted to draw as much attention to the TARA dilemma as possible in hopes of gaining optimum support.

After about six weeks, Gandhi and Ali set sail for their return to Africa. While aboard, they received word that Lord Elgin has issued a statement from L.W. Ritch, saying that Lord Elgin had stated that he would not advise the Crown to approve the ordinance. The joy Gandhi and Ali felt over that development was not to last. Once they arrived in Cape Town, and even more so when they reached Johannesburg, they realized they had put too much stock in Ritch's message.

THE LETDOWN

The Indians did not take into account that although the Transvaal was at that time a Crown Colony and subservient to British rule, it was to become a protectorate of Responsible Government on January 1, 1907, meaning that the government of the Transvaal would be accountable to its own Parliament, rather than to the King of England. Lord Elgin apparently issued his statement against the Black Act, in agreement with Transvaal attorney Richard Solomon. Elgin told Solomon that the Transvaal could do what it pleased after the aforementioned date and, in effect, the Indians had not won at all. The implementation of TARA had only been postponed, and the Indians knew they had been tricked. When the Transvaal became a Responsible Government on March 21, 1907, the first item passed by its legislature was the budget and the second, TARA, in its original form. It would take effect on July 1, with all Indians required to register by July 31.

Indians of all ages began picketing the registration office as soon as it opened on July 1, and many articles were written by Gandhi in various publications, advising Indians not to comply with the government. To culminate all their resistance efforts, another meeting was called at the Pretoria Mosque on the July 31 deadline. General Louis Botha, who had fought the British and earned great respect in the Boer War, had been elected the Prime Minister of the Transvaal in March 1907. He sent William Hosken to reprimand the recalcitrant Indians on his behalf. Hosken was politely received and presented Botha's words: "The Indians have done all they could and have acquitted themselves like men. But now that their opposition has failed, and the law has been passed, the community must prove their loyalty and love of peace by submitting to it."[4]

The next speaker was Ahmad Muhammad Kachhalia, a Muslim who was well respected in the Transvaal. After calmly telling the crowd that though he had listened politely to Hosken, "I swear in the name of God that I will be hanged but I will not submit to this law, and I hope that every one present will do likewise."[5] At this, Gandhi wrote that his resolve had been strengthened. He also took personal responsibility for advising the Indian community to oppose the law.

When the deadline had passed, the government approved a one-month extension to the deadline and subsequently there were others. The government was waiting for the poorly financed Indian anti-registration campaign to self-destruct. However, that did not happen and, on November 30, the final deadline passed. Only about 500 of the 13,000 Indians living in the Transvaal had registered, and the government decided that it was time to take further action.

Gandhi wrote that because of this blatant snubbing of authority, the government decided to arrest someone. Rama Sundra, a resident of Germiston, some nine miles from Johannesburg, was adamant about not registering with the government and spoke his views openly in a few animated speeches. Enemies of Sundra talked to the Asiatic Department about his open contempt for the new law and suggested that if Sundra were arrested, more Indians would register as required. Soon afterward, Sundra was arrested. Because this was the initial arrest in the Satyagraha campaign, there was uproar within the South African Indian community and Sundra became a national figure. He was put on trial and sentenced to one month in prison.

Even though one might think this would be demoralizing to the Indian population of South Africa, Sundra's sentencing had the opposite effect. A large proportion of the Indian population was ready to go to jail to preserve their human rights. Fewer Indians registered because of Sundra's arrest, and when he was released from prison, hundreds came out to wish him well and to feast in his honor. Yet Sundra was broken by the time he spent in jail, which had been too lonely an experience for him. Regardless of the support he was shown upon his release, he ended up leaving the Transvaal and the movement. As it turned out, Sundra was in reality an indentured servant who never completed his term of service. (To Indians, breaking of a contract was detestable.) In spite of his darkened past, Sundra had given impetus to the movement. However, arrests continued.

WELCOMING PRISON

Gandhi and several of his compatriots, along with members of the Chinese community, was given notice to appear in court on December 28, 1907, to explain why they had not registered with the Asiatic Department as ordered by law and to give reason why they should not be ordered from the Transvaal within 48 hours. Each case was conducted individually, but none of the charged could answer the court successfully and all were ordered out of the Transvaal within the preordained time limit, which would expire on January 10, 1908. When the group did not obey by this date, they were required to present themselves for sentencing.

Gandhi had news that members of the Indian community had been sentenced to three months' imprisonment at hard labor, plus they had been levied a hefty fine. If unable to pay the fine, the sentence was extended to six months. Because Gandhi had been one of the organizers of the movement, he told the magistrate that he should receive an even heavier sentence; however, the judge did not agree and sentenced him to two months' imprisonment, without labor. Gandhi was taken to the Johannesburg jail.

Gandhi was told to remove his clothing and was given prison clothing to wear, which was filthy after being worn by other prisoners before him. The dirtiness disturbed his personal need for cleanliness, but Gandhi donned the outfit, nonetheless. It had been decided before any sentencing began that the members of the Satyagraha movement would follow all the rules their jailers set down, without contempt, as long as the policies did not impinge on their self-respect or their religious beliefs. Gandhi was then led to a cell where the others who were sentenced with him were being held, and all were delighted that they would spend their time of imprisonment together. Outside, people paraded with black flags; some were flogged for their civil disobedience.

In the days following Gandhi's imprisonment, many of the Satyagrahis were arrested for failure to produce a permit when asked to do so by a police officer, and within a week, more than 100 prisoners were in the cell. Eventually, all new prisoners were sentenced not only to jail time, but to hard labor, as in Pretoria. The population was swelling to 150 men, and the authorities were becoming frustrated, while the cells became even more stinking and filthy. Many men became ill and several of the prisoners were forced to sleep outdoors.

Two weeks into his jail term, Gandhi was visited by Albert Cartwright of the *Transvaal Leader*, who as a sympathizer with the Indian condition and a friend of Gandhi's was sent to negotiate some type of settlement for the government. He had a rough draft of a commitment from Field Marshal and Cabinet Minister Jan Christian Smuts, another Boer War hero and Botha's right-hand man. Gandhi found Smuts' proposal vague and unacceptable and made changes to the deal. Cartwright did not approve of Gandhi's changes and told Gandhi that General Smuts had considered the agreement final. To this, Gandhi replied, "General Smuts need not confront us with an ultimatum, saying that these terms are final. He has already aimed one pistol in the shape of the Black Act at the Indians. What can he hope to gain by aiming a second?"[6] At that, Cartwright agreed to present Gandhi's conditions to the General.

MEETING THE ADVERSARY

As new prisoners were arrested, Gandhi and the others received news from outside. Gandhi knew that the Indian community was behind him, as they had allowed him full authority in making any acceptable agreement in their cause. With that knowledge, Gandhi and two of the other prisoners signed the agreement and returned it to Cartwright for Smuts's approval.

Two days later, on January 30, 1908, Gandhi was taken to meet General Smuts, and they had a long discussion. Smuts told Gandhi that Cartwright had presented their revisions to the agreement and complimented Gandhi on his and the other Indians' resolve even while still imprisoned. He also told Gandhi that he had no animosity toward the Indians and that he was also a barrister. He had discussed the altered agreement with Prime Minister Botha, who agreed to the Indians' terms. Smuts said that TARA would be repealed as soon as most of the Indians had voluntarily registered with the Asiatic Department. He also told

Gandhi that he would send him the redrafted bill regarding registration when it was ready for Gandhi's criticism and that he wanted no further trouble with the Indian community. He immediately freed Gandhi and told him that he would phone the prison and tell the guards to release the other prisoners the following morning.

But his last comments upset Gandhi. Smuts asked that there be no more meetings or demonstrations that would put the government in a bad light. Gandhi countered by saying that he had to hold meetings to advise the Indian people about the settlement, what it meant to them, and how it was achieved. To this, Smuts agreed, saying that he knew Gandhi understood his meaning.

Upon his return to Johannesburg, Gandhi immediately called an emergency midnight meeting regarding the settlement with the government. First, he explained the terms of the agreement to a few of the prominent merchants. Most were satisfied with what had transpired, but some worried that Smuts had not made the agreement in good faith. They feared that when most of them were registered, Smuts would renege on his promised to rescind TARA. They argued that the act should be repealed first, and then Indians could voluntarily register. Gandhi saw merit in their case.

However, he explained to the merchants that although their arguments had value, Satyagrahis should never be afraid and never fear to trust an opponent, even if the opponent breaks that trust many times over. By speculating that trust in the government might play into the government's hands, they were ignoring the principles of Satyagraha. Even if the government did break its promise, Gandhi believed that the community still had recourse. He said, "Suppose we register voluntarily, but the Government commits a breach of faith and fails to redeem its promise to repeal the Act. Could we not then resort to Satyagraha?"[7] With this, Gandhi had satisfied most of the Satyagrahi merchants' concerns; however, he had no idea what the impending meeting would bring.

After explaining the agreement to the crowd, and overcoming the objections that the merchants presented earlier, a Pathan, a tribesman from what is now the northeastern Pakistan/Afghanistan region, stood up to criticize Gandhi for agreeing to the fingerprinting portion of the law.[8] Gandhi said that he would be willing to give his fingerprints, but that anyone not willing to provide them should abstain. The Pathans reminded Gandhi that fingerprinting was his central argument in encouraging them to refuse to register at the start.

Gandhi responded by saying that by using fingerprinting as the central argument against TARA, he was able to rouse the crowd more quickly.

To Gandhi, circumstances had changed. Whereas provision of fingerprints would certainly have been a crime against the people before the circumstances of the law had changed, he saw complying with the subsequent law as a mark of the gentlemen's agreement.

With that, the Pathan cried out that he had learned that Gandhi had accepted £15,000 from Smuts to accept the agreement and that he would slay, in the name of Allah (God), the first man that registered. To that, Gandhi chastised the Pathan for threatening violence in the name of God. He also said that he would never sell the community out and rested on his reputation. He went further in insisting to be the first man to register and told the Pathan that if he intended to carry out his warning, Gandhi should be the target.

After this exchange, a meeting official reiterated the need for Indians to come to agreement about the proposed amendments to the law. Aside from dissention from a few Pathans, the resolution to accept the agreement passed overwhelmingly and, the following morning, Gandhi went to see to the prisoners released.

VIOLENCE IN A PEACEFUL MOVEMENT

On February 10, 1908, the reregistration forms were ready for the voluntary registration to begin, with the wording changed to meet with the Asians' approval. When Gandhi arrived at his office that morning, he ran into a former client, Mir Alam, and some Pathan companions. Gandhi greeted Alam, but the man was grim. When Gandhi set out for the registration office, Alam asked where he was going. Gandhi replied that he was going to register and give his fingerprints. He asked Alam to accompany him and said that he would secure the registration form and a thumbprint card so that Alam could register with only providing his two thumbprints, rather than those for all 10 fingers. With that, Gandhi was struck unconscious by a blow to the back of his head, and the assailants continued to beat and kick him while he lay on the ground. When Gandhi's companions tried to stop the men from beating Gandhi, blows were heaped on them, as well. The assaulters fled, but they were later caught and arrested.

When Gandhi regained consciousness, he was told that his assailants were in custody. Joseph Doke, who was then editor of *The Indian Opinion*, leaned over him and offered his residence as a place to recover. Gandhi accepted, but while waiting to be transported, Mr. Chamney, the Registrar of Asiatics arrived. Gandhi insisted that he bring the papers for registration so that he would be first to register, as he had promised. Chamney tried to dissuade the injured man, saying there was plenty of time for him to register, but Gandhi was adamant and Chamney provided the papers for him.

Gandhi had lacerations on his cheek and lip and a nasty gash on his ribs, which were tended to by a physician. Gandhi's injuries were not serious, but the doctor instructed him not to speak until the stitches from his ribs were removed, so Gandhi wrote a short note to the Satyagrahis, asking them to be tolerant of those who disagreed and to forgive the men who had attacked him. After about 10 days and constant nursing from the Dokes, Gandhi was well enough to leave their home.

His next action surprised all but his closest associates. Gandhi wrote to the Attorney General, asking him to release the men who had attacked him. However, his wishes were overridden by the Europeans in the community. They wrote their own letter saying that regardless of Gandhi's wishes, the assailants should be prosecuted and they were willing to provide evidence in the case. After such insistence, Mir Alam and one of his companions were tried, found guilty, and sentenced to hard labor for three months for their crime.

At the Phoenix Settlement, Gandhi's family naturally worried about his condition. Gandhi wanted to see them to allay their fears. He had also received news of negative sentiment regarding the settlement popping up in Durban, and Gandhi thought it necessary to return to Natal. Although TARA affected only those Indians living in the Transvaal, Gandhi knew that the fight would have repercussions for all Indians in South Africa. By returning, he hoped to soothe worried minds in all corners.

A meeting of the Natal Indians was called upon Gandhi's arrival; however, advisors told him not to attend because they feared he might be attacked again. Yet Gandhi saw himself as a servant of the public. Just as a servant is considered disobedient if he does not come when called, neither would Gandhi be obedient to the cause if he did not appear. He thought that a servant should not fear his master and that he should be willing to accept accolades as well as blame. For those reasons, he attended the meeting against all advice to the contrary.

Gandhi outlined the situation in the Transvaal for the audience and told the crowd of its implications for the Natal community. He was ready to end his speech when a Pathan rushed the stage with a club. At that instant, someone turned off the lights, and Gandhi escaped the attack. While the chairman of the meeting tried to quell the crowd, Parsi Rustomji went to the police. Superintendent Alexander sent a squad of police officers to the scene, and they ushered Gandhi away and to Rustomji's home for protection, once again.

The next morning, Rustomji met with the Pathans in the community and asked them to present their grievances against Gandhi. They would offer no particulars, only that they knew Gandhi had betrayed them. Gandhi saw no sense in meeting with them. Their minds had been made up, and until he proved himself to the Pathans again, there was no point in arguing. Without addressing their claims, Gandhi set off for the Phoenix Settlement, but with an entourage. Jack Moodaley, a Tamil boxer, and several others insisted on accompanying Gandhi as his bodyguards. Moodaley and the other men stood watch over Gandhi until they arrived at Phoenix.

Gandhi used his time at the settlement to write a long description of the agreement made with the authorities regarding TARA for *The Indian Opinion*. It was an imaginary discussion involving questions and answers to make the entire situation clearer, not just for those in Natal but for those in the Transvaal, as well. The imaginary discourse was so successful in helping the Indians in the Transvaal understand that most of them voluntarily registered quickly, so quickly, in fact, that the registration office had trouble keeping up with the work. Soon, the Indian part of the bargain made with Smuts was fulfilled.

However, the government's end of the deal was never met. Not only was the legislation kept on the books, but more provisions were made to ensure that the voluntary registrations made after the deadline were legal. By late May, 7,000 of the 9,000 Indians in the Transvaal had registered voluntarily, and Smuts issued a warning saying that after June 9, any unregistered Asiatic would be subject to the old law. Registration would be forced, or they would be expelled from the country immediately.

When the Satyagrahis heard the news, many admonished Gandhi with "I told you so." Smuts was well-known for saying one thing and doing another, but Gandhi had made the bargain with him in good faith. Now, Gandhi's close associates asked him how the people could ever believe Smuts again. Gandhi replied that it was not belief in Smuts that was at issue, but trust, and said that it was every man's duty to trust his fellow man. He said that if the Satyagrahis only remained true to themselves, others would not be found wanting.

Gandhi quickly wrote a letter to Smuts, remarking that the newly proposed bill was a breach of their agreement. When Smuts did not reply, Gandhi spoke with Albert Cartwright, who said that Smuts could not be forced to reply via the press, but that he would do what he could to help. Gandhi also wrote an article in *The Indian Opinion* titled "Foul Play?" regarding the situation. Still, he received no further communication from Smuts. Gandhi had thought that the major upheaval of the original

Satyagraha struggle would end with the settlement. What he did not envision was that the Satyagraha struggle was not nearing its conclusion. It had only begun.

NOTES

1. Ashe, *Gandhi*, p. 105.
2. Gandhi, *Satyagraha in South Africa*, p. 74.
3. Ashe, *Gandhi*, p. 100.
4. Gandhi, *Satyagraha in South Africa*, p. 85.
5. Gandhi, *Satyagraha in South Africa*, p. 86.
6. Gandhi, *Satyagraha in South Africa*, p. 99.
7. Gandhi, *Satyagraha in South Africa*, p. 102.
8. Most Pathans are Sunni Muslims. Only about 50 were in the Transvaal in 1908, having come to South Africa as soldiers during the Boer War.

Chapter 8

AN END TO SATYAGRAHA IN SOUTH AFRICA

Indians in South Africa and in India were furious at the government's neglect in upholding the terms of the agreement made between Gandhi and Smuts. In the Transvaal, registration certificates were voluntarily surrendered with the intention of burning them en masse in a giant bonfire. The government had drawn a line that Indians were willing to cross, knowing well that their disobedience would mean imprisonment. Commitment to Satyagraha had been turned into obstinacy for the cause, and an ultimatum was issued. Either the act would be repealed or the certificates would be burned and civil disobedience on a grand scale would ensue. This challenge provoked the legislators, who passed the bill without hesitation.

On August 16, 1908, a meeting of Satyagrahis was held on grounds of the Hamidia Mosque in Johannesburg, and it was set to begin two hours after the legislature made its decision. The intention was to inform the crowd of the outcome, which they would receive via wire, and in case of the bill's passage, to burn the registration certificates that had been collected. In anticipation of the worst, a giant black cauldron with four legs had been purchased and set on a platform in one corner of the area. The balance of the space was filled with Indians from every caste and origin. Just as the meeting was to begin, a runner came with telegram in hand to proclaim that the government had passed the new restrictions and a roar went up. Gandhi thought it was because the people were all anxious to show the government their disdain for the entire registration debacle.

When the meeting opened, the first thing Gandhi did was to advise the crowd that those wanting their certificate back should take it. He told them that merely burning the paper did not constitute a crime; however, anyone who secured a replacement registration certificate after the act would be dishonorable. Taking the certificate back beforehand carried no shame, but to commit and then back down would be harmful to the community and to the cause. No certificate returns were requested, and more than 2,000 certificates were thrown into the cauldron, saturated with paraffin, and lit. Others, who had not already surrendered their papers, went to the cauldron and added theirs to the flames.

News of the Indians' actions spread rapidly. Many reporters had been to the meeting, and one sent a story off to the London *Daily Mail*, comparing the meeting with the Boston Tea Party in America. But TARA was not the only legislation spurring the Indians to revolt. In 1907, Smuts had introduced the Transvaal Immigration Act, No. 15, which imposed a proficiency test on all entering the Transvaal, except indentured laborers. Although it appeared to have a general influence, the act was aimed at keeping Indians out and was also at issue. The Satyagrahis decided that not only TARA, but the Immigration Act as well, should be addressed by the community.

To this end, Gandhi began a series of letters with General Smuts. He told him that the Indians were upset by not only TARA, but the Immigration Act as well. Smuts replied that many Europeans had come to sympathize with the Satyagrahis but that they did not know Gandhi as well as he did. He wrote that Gandhi exploited the leniency he had been given, gaining an inch but wanting a mile, and for that reason, he would not advocate repeal for any of the legislation. He accused Gandhi of cunning, although Gandhi could not understand his argument. Gandhi reasoned that he could not have protested legislation that had not existed before meeting Smuts and that Smuts only knew him in terms of opposing such legislation. A series of circuitous arguments were traded back and forth; Gandhi concluded that the struggle was only intensifying. Neither side could concede.

To strengthen their two-pronged attack, the Satyagrahis then decided to test the Immigration Act by bringing in an Indian who would satisfy the requirements of the act. If the Indian was thrown into jail anyway, it would prove the legislation discriminatory. One part of the act said that anyone who was not conversant in a European language would be prohibited. A Parsi man by the name of Sorabji Shapurji Adajania, who knew English but had not been to the Transvaal before, was selected. He would go to England, take the necessary steps to be called to the bar, and take Gandhi's place in service to the community when he returned to South Africa. During his stay in England, Sorabji became friendly with Gokhale.

He was influential among the students there and seemed to have been the perfect choice to test the law.

Sorabji returned to the Transvaal, after alerting the government that he fully intended to test the Immigration Restriction Act. The immigration officer knew Sorabji and said there was no question that he knew English, as his European language. Sorabji replied that he should be tested or arrested, whichever the government intended. Sorabji entered the Transvaal without his registration certificate and without conflict. He continued to Johannesburg where he wrote to the police superintendent that it was his intention to remain in the Transvaal, that he had ordinary knowledge of English, and that he would subject himself to testing when the government so desired to test him. He made no mention of registering with the state. Rather than a reply, Sorabji received a summons to appear before the court.

FIRST TO BE ARRESTED

On Wednesday, July 8, 1908, Sorabji appeared in court, represented by Gandhi, who asked for an immediate dismissal because the summons was defective. The judge ruled for the defendant and Sorabji was released, but with the admonishment to reappear before the court on Friday, July 10. On that date, Sorabji was ordered to leave the Transvaal within seven days, and on July 20, when he did not register and remained in the country, he was sentenced to a one-month imprisonment at hard labor. This only steeled the Indians' resolve to oppose the laws.

To increase the pressure, it was decided that two groups of Indians from Natal would come to the Transvaal. One group had lived in the Transvaal before and had some knowledge of English. The second group had never lived in the Transvaal but knew English well. Among the two groups were Sheth Daud Mahomed, president of the Natal Indian Congress; Parsi Rustomji, a prominent businessmen who had previously lived in the Transvaal; and Surendra Medh, Pragji Khandubhai Desai, Ratansi Mulji Sodha, and Gandhi's own son, Harilal, who had all been formally educated. When the men arrived at the Transvaal border on August 18, the entire group was arrested, put before a judge, and told to leave the Transvaal within seven days. When they ignored the order, they were arrested again at Pretoria on August 28 and deported; however, they returned on August 31. On September 8, they were sentenced to three months at hard labor.

The whole scenario delighted the Transvaal Indians, and they decided to perform acts of disobedience in hopes of imprisonment. One way was to leave and reenter the Transvaal without proper registration. Although they were already citizens of the country, they had burned their registration papers and could not produce them for police. The second way was to pursue business, as trading without registration permits was illegal. Indians continued to pour into the Transvaal from Natal, as well, and refused to register with immigration. Indians of all social classes and ages were sentenced and jailed for terms of a few days to three months, and although the labor their jailers meted out to them was indeed hard and often disgusting, they performed assigned tasks cheerfully. Even Gandhi was thrown into jail again, although he was separated from the other prisoners. He spent his term at Pretoria jail, in solitary confinement, and was taken outside only twice a day for exercise.

So many Indians were arrested and jailed that the government began to consider the expense. Although they had the option of deportation, their customary action was to put the offenders outside the Transvaal borders and to leave them, whence it was quite easy to reenter the country. Ultimately, the government sent the arrestees back to India at great inconvenience. They were sent on steamers as deck passengers, and the sustenance from the government was poor and inadequate. Besides, many were born in South Africa and had never even been to India. Though loyal to the cause, the prospect of losing all they had in South Africa daunted some Satyagrahis and weakened their resolve. Some acquired new registrations with the government rather than face total bankruptcy. The government kept its hard line on prisoners, as well, and men started to die in jail. Many fell away from the fight, but many remained stalwart, regardless of the consequences.

The government had no idea what to do. Officials arrested, deported, and abused as many Indians as they could, and nothing worked to quell the uprising. Court cases were not always successful, and each time the government lost a case, it strengthened the Indians' resolve. Aside from endangering their positions, those who had backed away from committing punishable offenses were still active with the cause and continued their help by donating money or performing clerical tasks. Gandhi held no animosity toward them and was grateful for their continued support.

During this time, the countries in South Africa were working toward an alliance and planned to send a deputation to England to present their proposals. As restrictions affecting Indians were becoming more prominent in each of the separate states, the Satyagrahis knew this consolidation of power would do them no good. It was decided that Gandhi would again make a pilgrimage to England. When he left on the *S. S. Kenilworth Castle* from Cape Town on June 23, 1909, Sheth Haji Habib, a Muslim merchant was with him. Habib was not a Satyagrahi, but his sentiments lay with them. General Smuts was already in England, and another deputation from Natal went at the same time.

Once the deputation arrived, they met with Lord Amphill, who had ties to General Botha. He brought them a message, stating that they were not willing to repeal any of the legislation or eradicate the discrimination, blaming the European community, who would not allow it even if they were in that frame of mind. They agreed to give in to small demand but also gave Gandhi a warning: "If you ask for more you will only be inviting trouble for yourself as well as for your people."[1] Amphill said that he understood Gandhi's position, but they remained at odds over the issue, while remaining friendly.

A NEW DIRECTION FOR INDIA

While in England, Gandhi noticed that the unrest and push toward Indian home rule had intensified. In 1905, the Indian National Congress had first begun discussing the future of India as an independent nation, and in 1906, the All-India Muslim League was founded. Yet, what spurred seriousness of purpose was the partition of East and West Bengal in 1905, which the English described as purely necessary for the area's administration. Generally, the Muslims living in the eastern portion, Assam, saw this as recognition of their differences with the Hindu population of the western side. However, the Bengali Hindus saw it as a contrivance for strangling an independence movement that had sprung up there. In accord with the Hindu-run Indian National Congress, a campaign of *Swadeshi* (being an advocate of one's own country) was organized, characterized by the boycott of English goods with an increase in the production of Indian goods to satisfy the demand.

Gandhi, in his own fight in South Africa, had not realized the intensity the idea of home rule had gained, but while in England, he saw the full effects. On his way back to South Africa, he wrote another booklet—"*Hind Swaraj*" or "Home Rule" —to explain the movement. It would be published in *The Indian Opinion* on his return to South Africa. Gandhi claims to have written the booklet to demonstrate the importance of Satyagraha and its tenets of nonviolent resistance. Support for the movement was on his mind because it was uncertain how much time would be needed to prove its efficacy; however, it was not monetary support that had him concerned. He worried about the character of the individuals involved in the movement and whether they could sustain their fervor over time. Up to that time, the needs of each jailed Satyagrahi were evaluated and each of their families was supported by the movement accordingly. The funds needed to continue such support would be considerable over time, and Gandhi discerned the need to establish another commune. Phoenix was unsuitable. It was quite far from Johannesburg—a journey of 300 miles. Gandhi thought it was important to secure alternate quarters in the Transvaal.

Hermann Kallenbach, a German architect who had come to South Africa during World War I, sympathized with the Satyagraha movement and assisted whenever he could. He purchased a farm of 1,100 acres, about 21 miles from Johannesburg, and gave it to Gandhi and the Satyagrahis to use, free of charge. The property held about 1,000 fruit trees; a small house, which was able to hold about six people; and a spring and two wells from which to draw potable water. The leaders decided to build houses on the farm in which the families of the jailed and free Satyagrahis could settle. It would be known as Tolstoy Farm, where all of the work was done by manual labor. Two block houses were built, one to house 60 men and another for 10 women. They built a separate house for their benefactor, Kallenbach, a schoolhouse, a carpenter's shop, and a shoemaker's shop, among other structures.

On October 22, 1912, Gokhale landed at Cape Town, South Africa. He was not in perfect health, and Gandhi's rigorous schedule for him had to be curtailed somewhat, although Gokhale protested. A banquet was held in his honor in Johannesburg, and most of the attendees were Europeans. At this gathering, Gokhale made what he saw as his most important speech in South Africa regarding repudiation of the £3 tax and TARA. While in Johannesburg, he also addressed a mass meeting of Indian expatriates and also traveled to Natal. He concluded his visit in Pretoria, where he would meet with Generals Botha and Smuts. Because of the recent history of the Satyagraha movement, it had been decided that Gandhi would not attend to avoid animosity. However, Gokhale did ask Gandhi to prepare a concise briefing on recent events. He also asked Gandhi to provide him with a statement of how far the Satyagrahis were prepared to go to have their demands met.

The meeting with Gokhale, Botha, and Smuts lasted two hours, and Gokhale returned with good news. He assured Gandhi that TARA would be rescinded, there would be no further restrictions on immigration, and that the £3 tax would be repealed. After former dealings with the generals, Gandhi was not at all optimistic that the promises made to Gokhale would be kept; yet, Gokhale remained firm in his convictions. He told Gandhi that he would accept no excuses for Gandhi's returning to India within one year and left South Africa on November 17, 1912.

Gokhale's visit to South Africa strengthened the Satyagrahis' resolve. It also strengthened their position by including abolition of the £3 tax in their list of grievances. Moreover, the visit gave Gokhale greater authority in India when the South African problem arose in the Indian National Congress. He was able to further the cause by sparking Indians in the homeland to protest on their fellow countrymen's behalf. This resulted in an increase in funding to help the Satyagrahis' mission progress.

The Satyagrahis were careful not to involve those not directly affected by the laws they were protesting. Only those living in the Transvaal, for instance, were recruited to protest TARA. Gandhi also made certain, as has been seen, not to involve every grievance, but to only tackle one problem at a time. Only TARA was in question until subsequent restrictions arose in its wake, and the £3 tax was not included until Gokhale's visit when the Generals made promises regarding the levy.

ANOTHER BETRAYAL

At the Union Parliament session after the departure of Gokhale, Smuts declared that European residents of Natal had opposed repeal of the £3 tax and as such, there would be no action taken regarding the issue, though Smuts might have presented the bill to the Assembly and allowed it to take its course. The Satyagrahis saw this as blatant squelching of the promise, tantamount to an approval for reaction. In the Satyagrahis' eyes, Smuts's action was a personal effrontery to Gokhale and the nation of India, which had to be answered, and the ranks of Satyagrahis was swelling with the inclusion of all indentured servants, burdened by the £3 tax.

Another new surge of protestors entered the cause at that time, as well: the Satyagrahi women. They had wanted to enter the conflict when their husbands were arrested, but the men felt it was wrong to sacrifice their women to the cause; moreover, it was a masculinity issue, as they saw the oppressive laws to be directed only at men. Of course, whole families were affected by the restrictions in that the men could not provide for their families while in jail or when hurt or injured because of their protests. The women and children also suffered emotionally. Yet, a situation arose to assuage the men's minds.

On March 14, 1913, the Cape Supreme Court ruled that any marriage outside Christianity and/or not recorded by the Registrar of Marriages was invalid. Indian marriages were not required to be registered by any government and were considered lawful and righteous by the religious ceremonies they observed. Indian marriages were, by an overwhelming majority, of Hindu, Muslim, and Parsi faiths. Thus, not only marriages that had taken place in South Africa, but also those that had occurred in India were thereby voided. Indian men saw their wives relegated to the level of mistress and their children become illegitimate. The women were as furious as their husbands were.

Gandhi wrote a letter to government officials, explaining the situation, and asked whether the Supreme Court had interpreted the law correctly. The quick reply was negative, and a quick decision was made to pursue Satyagraha against the newest insult, which was perhaps more harsh than any, as it involved the Satyagrahis' women. Not only were women welcomed into the ranks of protestors, but they were encouraged to join in the activities that courted prison, as well. Although they were sure to reap the same punishments as the men had in the past, they were stalwart and did not falter in giving the cause their full support. The first female Satyagrahis came from the Tolstoy Farm. They wanted to be arrested to garner the outrage of Indians on both continents.

First, they entered the Transvaal without permits, but no one arrested them. As it was illegal to sell anything without a permit there, they launched into trading, still without success. Gandhi came up with a plan to have all the residents of the Phoenix Settlement arrested, except for those needed to keep the camp and *The Indian Opinion* running and the children tended. Sixteen people in all were sent to the Transvaal, without permits, where they were sure to be arrested. Gandhi told them not to give name or address, which was a separate offense and punishable by imprisonment. He did not want the officers to know some of their names for fear that they would be ignored once it was realized they were part of Gandhi's family. At the same time, the women from the Tolstoy Farm were to enter Natal, where it was by then an offense to enter without registration, as well. If they were not arrested, they were to go to Newcastle, where there were many indentured laborers in the coalmines, and to encourage them to strike. Government officials were sure to arrest them for inciting the strike, along with the striking laborers.

When Gandhi approached the women of the Phoenix Settlement with his plan, he assured them there was no obligation. They could join or not join, but he wanted them to know the consequences if they did so and gave them some time to consider the implications of the plot. When it came to Kasturba, Gandhi was reluctant to approach her. He knew that she would think she had to obey his wishes when he wanted her to be certain to take the steps toward Satyagraha on her own. Kasturba heard her husband talking with the other women, who expressed their desire to fight against the government regardless of the costs, and was insulted. She said, "What defect is there in me which disqualifies me for jail?"[2] He reminded her that if he asked, she might feel obliged to go just because she was his wife. She told him emphatically that she was bound, not by marriage but by conscience, to join the struggle.

When the Phoenix residents reached the border of the Transvaal and refused to give their names and addresses, they were arrested and, on September 23, 1913, sentenced to three months in jail at hard labor. The women from the Transvaal were not arrested on entering Natal and progressed to Newcastle, where they incited the miners to strike. On hearing the news, Gandhi left at once to join them. On October 21, 1913, the women from the Transvaal were arrested and sentenced to three months in prison at hard labor and went to the same prison as the women from the Phoenix Settlement. All Indians, both in South Africa and in India, were horrified by the turn of events. The women suffered the same hardships as the men had before them, and one, who came out of jail with a high fever, died a few days after her release.

MARCH TO THE TRANSVAAL

When Gandhi arrived in Newcastle, he heard horrible stories from the miners. Their employers had not only evicted them but punished them physically. All of these insults were taken in the spirit of Satyagraha and not returned in kind. Yet, Gandhi knew that the hardships were dire and could continue indefinitely. His solution was for the miners to discontinue reliance on their employers and to set off like pilgrims. Yet, thousands of people were involved and Gandhi had no idea how to support them. He instructed the workers to sell what possessions they could and to leave all else behind. He told them to come with only the clothes on their backs and a blanket. He vowed to live with them and to have meals with them for as long as the strike lasted. He also gave encouragement to those who were unable to follow this lifestyle, saying that no one was to rebuke them for their inability to cope.

The people lived outside with Gandhi, under the sky. The traders of Newcastle, who could not house Gandhi or their brethren for fear of reprisal and ruin, were anxious to help by other means and contributed cooking pots and food. Their gifts far exceeded Gandhi's expectations. Those who were unable to donate volunteered time and assistance.

The group living with Gandhi was enormous and without work, so it was inevitable that there would be trouble among them. However, for the days they continued this lifestyle, all was peaceful. Yet, Gandhi thought the tranquility was bound to end and came up with a new plan. He decided to take his "army" to the Transvaal and to have them cross the border, just as the people from the Phoenix Settlement had done. They decided to walk the 36 miles to the border, as the price of passage via rail for 5,000 people was prohibitive.

While preparing for the journey, Gandhi was summoned by the mine owners at Durban. He did not expect overwhelming results but accepted their invitation to hear what they had to say. He found the meeting to be an interrogation, rather than a negotiation, and he answered their questions suitably. He encouraged them to prevail upon the government to repeal the £3 tax, but they could not understand what they had to do with any governmental legislation. Gandhi replied that the strike was the only recourse they had to unfair treatment by the government and involved the mine owners, as they wanted men to work as indentures, rather than as free men. Gandhi refused to allow the miners to return to work, and the owners threatened him with "consequences," not for himself but for the striking workers. He replied that they knew their position and accepted it willingly. When Gandhi returned to Newcastle, he relayed the mine owners' threats, and advised the miners that they were free to return to the mines, if they feared reprisals. He also described the hardships of prison, but the men renewed their pledge to Gandhi to stay by his side.

The march to the Transvaal border began on October 29, 1913 with a daily ration of a pound and a half of bread and an ounce of sugar for each marcher. They were to accept any punishment that might be meted out to them, without retaliation, and to allow themselves to be arrested. Gandhi also told them that the march must continue if he were to be detained himself; he appointed a string of leaders who would take over as authority in succession if further arrests were made.

The caravan's first stop was at Charlestown, where traders provided shelter for some of the women and children and cooking outside the mosque. Merchants also supplied the pots and extra rice to add to the rice the group had brought along with them. Although claiming only to avert more hardship for his people, Gandhi wrote what might have been seen as a taunting letter to the government from Charlestown, in it, stating that his "army" intended to cross the border. He told officials to arrest them at Charlestown, rather than making them go the extra few miles. Two babies had been lost up to that point in the journey—one by exposure to the elements and the other to drowning when its mother dropped the infant in a stream she was crossing. But even the grieving mothers wanted to go on. Gandhi assured the government that if the £3 tax was repealed, the strike would be abandoned, and the miners would return to work. They would not be included in the Satyagrahis' other battles, as those grievances did not apply to them.

Gandhi waited for two days for a reply. When none was received, the troops continued onward. If they were not arrested, they would continue their march to Tolstoy Farm, where they would stay until the conflict was over. But before they left Charlestown, Gandhi made one final attempt at a settlement by phoning General Smuts. He assured the general's secretary that he would call off the strike and that any disturbances between Europeans and Indians along the way, as had been threatened, could be avoided by repeal of the £3 tax. General Smuts's secretary returned Smuts's message that he would have nothing to do with Gandhi. The next day, November 6, 1913, the marchers—2,037 men, 127 women, and 57 children—continued their journey.

GANDHI TRIED AND SENTENCED

When the army crossed the border of the Transvaal at Volksrust, a small contingent of mounted police was there to greet them, but it was obvious that they did not intend to make arrests. All members of the group crossed the border without incident and continued on their way. The first night in the Transvaal was spent at Palmford, about eight miles from the border.

That night, a police officer came to arrest Gandhi, who was permitted only to leave instructions with P. K. Naidoo, who had been sleeping nearby. Gandhi told Naidoo not to awaken anyone and to continue the march at sunrise. Only when the group stopped for lunch was he permitted to tell them what had happened to their leader. Gandhi was brought before a judge in Volksrust. As the prosecutor was not prepared for a trial, it was postponed for two weeks. Although the prosecutor protested, Gandhi was allowed to post £50 bail and was released. Kallenbach, who was in Volksrust with him, had a car waiting to return Gandhi to the marchers. A reporter from *The Transvaal Leader*, who later published the whole account, accompanied him. On November 8, Gandhi was arrested again at Sanderton. When he arrived at court, he saw that five of his coworkers had also been arrested. Although they were jailed, Gandhi was able to post another £50 and rejoin the march.

The government was confounded by the marchers' commitment to nonviolence. Had they rioted, it would have been easy for the government to send an army to contain the strikers with force. If the government allowed the marchers to reach Tolstoy Farm, their inactivity would be perceived as weakness. Whatever action officials took would have to be enacted before the marchers arrived at their destination.

On the November 9, Henry Polak, on his way to India to help Gokhale present the South African situation to the British and Indian governments, came to join the marchers at Gokhale's request. Because Polak was European, Gokhale thought that perhaps Polak was better able to negotiate with government officials, and Polak met the crowd at Teakwood. As Polak and Gandhi were leading the march that evening, the head immigration officer and a police officer met the group and arrested Gandhi again.

On the morning of the November 10, at Balfour, three special trains waited at the station to arrest all the marchers and deport them to Natal. At the behest of the appointed leaders, who reminded them that arrest was a goal of the march, all members of the group boarded the trains without incident. Gandhi was at the magistrate when this happened and knew nothing of the event. Once again, he asked for bail but was told the arrest warrant had come from another town. Gandhi would be transported there immediately. The charge was taking indentured laborers across the Natal border.

Polak had not been arrested and neither had Kallenbach, at first; however, officials changed their collective mind. Both men would be arrested and confined to the Volksrust jail. Gandhi was tried November 11 in Dundee, where he was convicted and sentenced to nine months in jail at hard labor. His second trial was still standing at Volksrust, where he met Kallenbach and Polak on November 13. The following morning, Gandhi was again convicted through a witness he himself furnished to ensure his conviction. Pleading guilty alone would not produce the desired effect, as no one could be imprisoned on a plea without witnesses. In turn, Gandhi testified against Kallenbach and Polak. All three were given three-month sentences.

The trio had hoped to serve their sentences together at Volksrust, but government officials decided to separate them. Gandhi went to prison in Bloemfontein in the capital of the Orange Free State, where fewer than 50 Indians lived, all serving as hotel waiters. Yet, he was happy to be among others, where he could study them and learn more about the world. The prison doctor was kind to him there and monitored his daily health by getting him the proper vegetarian foods. Polak was taken to Germiston jail and Kallenbach went to Pretoria.

THE AFTERMATH

The striking coal miners were left to a worse fate. Rather than house them in jails, where they would cost the government great expense, wire fences were erected around the mining compounds and the mine owners became the jailers. Now, the mine owners not only had labor, but slave labor, as the miners were forced back into the mines to complete the hard labor portion of their sentence, without remuneration of any kind. The miners revolted, though peacefully. They refused to work in the mines and were flogged for their behavior, but they would not budge. Each day, Gokhale received telegrams regarding the activities at the mines, and although he was grievously ill, he brought the South African trouble to the forefront of the mind of India.

At that point, Lord Hardinge, the Viceroy of India, came out against the actions of the South African government, although it was despicable for any member of the Realm to criticize any other arm of the government. He was berated in England for his position, but he continued to harangue the Transvaal Union Government and to praise the Satyagrahis for their nonviolent protest. He thus won the hearts of most Indians.

When Indian workers in other parts of South Africa learned of what was going on in Natal, they, too, joined the fray, against Gandhi's will. He knew there would be too many people to handle; yet, laborers in the north and south struck alongside their brethren. They sold their belongings to ensure their readiness for a protracted struggle. Volunteers arose to look after the crowds, as had happened in Natal, and the demonstration was peaceful—at least, on the side of the strikers. The government decided to be brutal.

Mounted military police not only stopped miners from leaving the mines but forced them back inside. When the crowd became unwieldy and threw stones at the officers, the police opened fire on the strikers and wounded or killed many. Still, not all of the laborers returned to work. Some of them ran away and hid themselves for fear of further reprisals.

Phoenix became the hub for strikers coming down from the north. Albert West, who had been running the English section of *The Indian Opinion* but had committed no punishable offense, was arrested. This sparked Gokhale to send men, who had donated heavily to the cause, from India. As European men of substance, their arrests would not be tolerated by Lord Hardinge. All waited for Smuts's next move.

Knowing that wrongs had been done, Smuts saw that the tax had to be repealed and there had to be admission of wrongdoing. Yet in fear of losing authority by doing these things outright, he established a three-man commission to examine the situation. The group's decisions would weigh heavily upon the government for any actions to be taken; however, the government was still the supreme authority. The council's first recommendations were to have all the Satyagrahis released and to appoint at least one Indian to the commission. The government acceded to the first suggestion and extended it further to include the release of Gandhi, Pollack, and Kallenbach, but it would not budge on the second.

When Gandhi was free again, the first thing he did was to write to Smuts, protesting his choice of committeemen, as two were known to be anti-Indian. Smuts wrote back to decline Gandhi's recommendations for other men who were neutral to the events unfolding, and to further curtail additions to the commission, stating it was for the benefit of the government, not the Indians. On December 1913, Gandhi published a notice to all Indians declaring that a party would leave Durban on January 1, with the express intent of being arrested, as he saw governmental actions as hedging. He did not believe that officials intended to repeal that tax or even to be fair with setting up the committee.

ANOTHER DEAL WITH SMUTS

Before January 1, Gandhi requested an interview with Smuts, and on his acceptance, the New Year's Day march was postponed. Gokhale and Lord Hardinge, however, encouraged Gandhi to forgo the march completely. They thought that the government was deliberating on Gandhi's demands and wanted him to wait, so as not to put Hardinge in an even more awkward position. Gandhi replied in a cable on December 24: "May you have strength during terrible crisis and may you find way out notwithstanding our inability recede."[3] After reading the cable, Gokhale and Lord Hardinge remained loyal to Gandhi's wishes.

When Gandhi went to meet General Smuts in Pretoria, Smuts was less arrogant than in the past. He would not give in on the idea of admitting a member of the Indian community to the council but said that the government was willing to grant the Satyagrahis' demands, providing they were recommended by the council. Until a determination was made, Smuts asked Gandhi to stop further action against the government concerning ill treatment of the marchers. Gandhi thought that the Satyagrahis had sworn to suffer, and in having done so had completed a part of their mission. Rather than destroy any chance of having their demands met, he decided to go along with Smuts, once again. Some of the Satyagrahis were unhappy with the decision, but when Gandhi explained the logic in it, most were willing to adhere to this new agreement.

To put the gist of their agreement into writing, Gandhi sent a new letter to Smuts, outlining the actions he expected the government to take and his agreement to suspend any further demonstrations. Smuts, in his reply, again stated that the government would await the recommendations of the commission. When the group's recommendations were handed down, they included acceptance of all the Satyagrahis' demands, including repeal of the £3 tax, the carryover of registration from one South African state to another, and the validation of Indian marriages. Parliament agreed to amend these issues, and the Satyagraha struggle in South Africa was over.

NOTES

1. Gandhi, *Satyagraha in South Africa*, p. 142.
2. Gandhi, *Satyagraha in South Africa*, p. 171.
3. M.K. Gandhi, *Collected Works of Mahatma Gandhi Online*, Vol. 13, "Cable to G.K. Gokhale," December 24, 1913, p. 437.

Chapter 9

FIRST STEPS TO FREEDOM

At the end of the Satyagraha struggle, Gokhale asked Gandhi to meet him in London before traveling home to India. After many speeches throughout South Africa, to explain the results of the Satyagraha struggle, Gandhi, Kasturba, and Hermann Kallenbach set sail for England in July 1914. Gandhi had recently fasted to atone for homosexual actions of two Satyagrahis, as he saw the sins of students the onus of teachers. Although he was not fully hale by the departure of his ship, he was sufficiently well to travel.

When the ship reached the English Channel, they learned that Great Britain had entered World War I on August 4. It took them two full days to reach Southhampton due to mines in the channel, which had to be navigated slowly and safely, and on landing, Gandhi learned that Gokhale was stranded in Paris, where he had gone for health reasons.

Still seeing himself as a citizen of the Realm, Gandhi called a meeting for Indians living in Great Britain and Ireland, to encourage young men to join the army. However, the Indians protested and did not want to be seen as slaves to the British any longer. Gandhi argued that they would win respect of the British if they were to stand with England in her time of need, and through his faith, many enlisted. Gandhi even wrote to Lord Crewe, then Secretary of State for the Colonies, offering his experience in forming another ambulance corps. After some hesitation, his invitation was accepted. After six weeks' training, a crew of eighty Indians was ready to serve, and many other Indians labored for the cause, making clothes and bandages for the wounded.

The Indian ambulance corps was under the assumption that Gandhi was to be their leader, but when they presented themselves for military training, another commanding officer was presented to them. They thought of him as their superior in military aspects of the job, with Gandhi remaining their leader in other matters, including discipline. However, this was not the case. The British officer took over the group entirely, and in only a few days, there was conflict between the British officer and the Indians.

To Gandhi's consternation, he was stricken then with an attack of pleurisy which is an inflammation of the pleura, the membrane that surrounds the lungs. He was forced to return home. With Gandhi gone, the British officer exercised his authority thoroughly and the men complained to Gandhi. They would have none of the officer's domineering and said they would not obey his orders any longer. When Gandhi approached the officer with the men's complaints, he was told to put the grievances in writing.

At the same time, many wounded soldiers arrived at Netley Hospital at Southhampton, which was built at the behest of nurse Florence Nightingale in 1896. Some of the Indian ambulance soldiers went to help at the hospital, while the others refused to serve. The Under Secretary of State for India called on Gandhi several times after this event, asking Gandhi to persuade the rest of the men to go to the hospital to aid the troops. His solution was that the Indians form a separate corps, under the authority of the hospital's Commanding Officer. As they would have no further dealing with the authoritarian officer, the men agreed and the balance of the corps went to Netley Hospital.

Because of the pleurisy, Gandhi was on a diet of plain brown bread, raw vegetables, and fruit. His care also included leaving the windows open for twenty-four hours, bathing in tepid water, oil massages, and fifteen to thirty-minute walks each day. The treatment improved Gandhi's health, but it did not bring him back to full vigor. After a while, it was determined that to cure himself, Gandhi must return to India.

RENEWING A LOVE OF INDIA

While onboard the ship steaming toward home, Gandhi began to feel much better, and after being away for ten years, he was happy to reach Bombay where he had a fine reception. The Phoenix families had come to India, where Gandhi had anticipated meeting them, except he had been detained in England because of the war and his illness. He spent the first few days trying to arrange suitable living quarters for them and, when he did, he thought they were happy and did not mind having left the Phoenix settlement. Gandhi stayed in Bombay a short while and then left for Poona. But before he left, the governor of Bombay, Lord Willingdon, sent for Gandhi and asked that he be informed before Gandhi took any steps concerning government. Gandhi agreed, as it was his duty as a Satyagrahi to understand the opposition first and to go along with their policies as far as he was able. Lord Willingdon assured Gandhi that his government would never willingly act in error.

Gandhi finally met up with Gokhale at Poona, where Gokhale had prepared another reception. During the party, Gandhi told his friend and mentor that he wanted to find another place to set up a commune with the people from the Phoenix Settlement. Gokhale thought it was a fine idea and even offered to fully fund the expenses of the ashram, which was a communal living arrangement, usually involving a religion group and its leader (guru). Gandhi was overwhelmed by his generosity, but Gokhale was overwhelmed by the gathering and fainted. He was whisked away but bade the participants to continue the fete.

After leaving Poona, Gandhi traveled to Rajkot and Porbandar, where he met his relatives. He had resumed his native Indian dress during the Satyagraha struggle in South Africa so that he could better relate to the indentured laborers. In England, he had sustained this manner of dress indoors, but in public, he wore a Kathiawar suit, consisting of a shirt, a dhoti, a jacket and a scarf, all made from cloth milled in India.

As Gandhi traveled through Kathiawar, he heard many complaints about restrictions put upon third-class passengers by customs officials. He read up on the matter and seeing merit in his countrymen's claims, he sought relief from Lord Willingdon, who had previously invited Gandhi's concerns. However, the Governor said that he could not help Gandhi, as he shifted the blame for the horrendous treatment on the leaders in Delhi. Willingdon advised Gandhi to seek relief from the government of India. Gandhi tried to reach someone of authority in the Indian government to no avail, but through persistence, he met Lord Chelmsford, the Viceroy. Chelmsford was surprised by Gandhi's claims and said he knew nothing of the circumstances. He agreed to look into the matter and, subsequently, third-class passenger restrictions were removed.

When Gandhi went to Shantiniketan in West Bengal, he found his Phoenix family living in harmony, headed by Maganlal Gandhi. Maganlal had done such a good job of substituting for Gandhi, of maintaining the rules and spirit of the Phoenix settlement, that everyone seemed re-adjusted to life in India and happy. Gandhi had been at

Shantiniketan for less than a week when he received news of Gokhale's death, and he left immediately for Poona.

Along the way, a colleague asked Gandhi whether Satyagraha would come to India. Gandhi replied that he had made a promise to Gokhale to travel in India for one year and to re-learn his homeland and what was going on inside it before giving any opinions. Gokhale had chuckled over some of Gandhi's published opinions in *Hind Swaraj* and said that after one year, Gandhi would rethink his positions.

FOUNDING A NEW PHOENIX

After Gokhale's funeral, Gandhi went on to Rangoon to visit Dr. Mehta and then on to the Kumbha fair at Hardvar, which is held only once every twelve years. He joined the Phoenix party, which was already there to offer assistance. It was during this festival that Gandhi realized how much his work in South Africa had affected the people of India. He spent most of his time holding discussions with the many people who sought him out for *darshan*, a sacred glimpse of the divine. This worship caused Gandhi to feel a great onus. He thought that the people expected too much of him and that they were following him blindly. He also began to feel the burden of burdening them, as everyone was constantly trying to cater to him. To assure he would not become the source of anyone else's discomfort, he made a vow never to eat more than five things each day and never to eat after dark. He continued to follow this rule throughout his life.

On his way home, Gandhi considered different locales to establish a permanent settlement. As he passed through Ahmedabad, friends encourage him to stay and offered not only to fund the expenses of the settlement, but promised a home for the settlers to live in. On May 20, 1915, the Satyagraha Ashram was founded in Ahmedabad, with twenty-five men and women living as a family. All began well, but trouble ensued with a Dalit family joined the group a few months later. With the strict Hindu ban against people of higher castes associating with the "Untouchables," all funding to the ashram stopped and a social boycott was threatened. Gandhi was prepared for this to happen, and when the money ran out for operating expenses, he told Maganlal they would have to move to the Dalit quarter of the city. While preparing to do so, a wealthy merchant drove up and approached Gandhi from his car. He asked Gandhi to meet him the next day at the same spot at the same time. When the car appeared, the merchant would not leave the vehicle but put enough money for a year's operating expenses into Gandhi's hand and drove away.

Gandhi's first political fight after returning to India surrounded the abolition of indentured servitude. In March 1916, a resolution was made in the Imperial Legislative Council to accomplish this, and it was accepted by Lord Hardinge, who announced that the British government had already agreed to end indenturing and that the legislation would take effect after wending its way through the system. However, this vague promise did not satisfy Gandhi, whose experience told him it was purposely cloudy; so, in February 1917, when a bill was introduced for the immediate abolition of indentured service and refused by the vice-chancellor, Gandhi knew it was time for Satyagraha. A meeting of the Imperial Citizenship Association was called and a deadline of July 31 was declared and resolved. At meetings all around India, resolutions were passed to comply with the same deadline. Yet, the agitation would never begin as the government declared that indentured emigration from India would end before July 31. Apparently, the government opted to avoid a larger battle by taking quick action on an issue that had already been decided.

Satyagraha would not be shelved for long, after Gandhi visited Champaran, Bihar in northern India, where mango and indigo plantations abound. Before his visit in 1917, he had never been to the area and had no idea how many people were involved in hard labor to bring the blue indigo dye to market. He went there at the behest of men, who complained of the harsh treatment they had received at the hands of the indigo planters, but before beginning any action, Gandhi intended to hear both sides of the issue. He interviewed many of the workers. When it was time to meet with the planters, he was rebuked by the Planter's Association secretary, who told him that he was an outsider and had no business intervening in the camps. When he called on the commissioner of that area, he was also threatened and told to leave the area. He knew that if he pursued his intended course of action, he would probably end up in jail, which could not daunt him.

Soon, he learned of a particular case of mistreatment and set off via elephant (a common transport in Champaran), to meet with the abused laborer. Less than halfway to the man's home, Gandhi and his associates were stopped by a messenger, who had a carriage with him. Gandhi was given the regards of the police superintendent, and he knew what that meant. He got into the carriage peacefully, was returned to his quarters, and told to leave the area. When he refused to sign a paper saying he had received the instruction, owing to the fact that he intended to stay and complete his purpose in Champaran, he was immediately issued a summons to appear in court the next day.

When Gandhi appeared at the courthouse, a crowd was waiting. The proceedings were handled amicably. Gandhi was made aware of the restrictions put upon him by the government, which he politely refused. Rather than vehement belligerence, Gandhi's spiritual passivity took over and the officials carried out their duties, while Gandhi carried out his. Governmental authority held no sway over Gandhi, nor did it daunt the people, who stood for a righteous cause.

The trial began with the court officials in an uproar. So many people were present, they worried that any actions against Gandhi would cause a riot, and so the Magistrate tried to postpone the case. Gandhi stopped this by saying that he wanted to plead guilty. He had disobeyed the order to leave the area and was ready to receive his just punishment. Still, the Magistrate postponed judgment. During the interim, Gandhi wired the Viceroy and other influential people the complete details of the case, and before he appeared for sentencing received word that the case had been dropped by order of the Lieutenant Governor. He was given liberty to proceed with his investigation and was told he could count on whatever help he needed from the local officials. Even Gandhi was surprised by the turn of events.

INDIGO BATTLES CONTINUE

As the planters were not obliged to abide by the same rules, they tried to make life difficult for Gandhi and his followers. Gandhi could not stay in anyone's quarters for fear of reprisals, so Gandhi and the oppressed workers set up camp in the open air. Dr. Mehta, stepped in and provided the necessary backing to finance the entire project.

Crowds of workers came to give testimony to Gandhi and each statement was written and examined closely for veracity. Representatives of the Criminal Investigations Department (C.I.D.) were present for each account, and although Gandhi might have protested, he saw their presence as positive in that the peasants seemed to exhibit more courage in reporting crimes committed by their employers without fear of retaliation. Gandhi had plenty of ammunition when he met with the planters, but he did not want to anger them. Some treated him with courtesy in kind, some were apathetic, while others were furious and treated him badly.

Gandhi was not only collecting statements, but in a short while was assessing the social situation among the workers. Sanitation was poor, there was inadequate health care, and the children had no teachers. It was not surprising, because of poverty; what the planters paid them was also a crime. The more statements Gandhi acquired from the people, the angrier planters became and they exerted their enormous influence on Bihar government officials.

In a letter from the government, Gandhi was asked if whether he was prolonging his inquiry and if perhaps, he should end it and leave Bihar. Gandhi replied that he would not leave Bihar until the people had been relieved of their torment. If the government saw to that, he would certainly leave the area.

After receiving Gandhi's letter, Sir Edward Gait, the Lieutenant Governor of Bihar, met with Gandhi and agreed to appoint an inquiry committee. He asked Gandhi to be one of its members. Gandhi agreed but wanted Gait to realize that even as a member of the committee, he would continue to be an advocate for the laborers and that if he was not satisfied by the committee's findings and the government's subsequent actions, he would advise the workers regarding their next steps. Gait accepted Gandhi's terms and a commission was formed.

Gait was obviously on the worker's side. He was influential in getting the committee to unanimously find for the workers and in the government's subsequent actions, which the planters protested vehemently. The system by which they controlled the labor force was found to be illegal and abolished. The workers were finally freed from the system that had virtually enslaved them.

Although Gandhi had wanted to remain in Bihar to help rehabilitate the workers and their families, he was soon summoned to Ahmedabad to take up a different, yet similar, cause. At the same time, he learned of a problem for the workers at Kheda, a Gujarat district bordering west Ahmedabad, who had been pressing for relief of taxation to no effect. Gandhi had learned of the situation before going to Ahmedabad but thought that the issue was clear-cut and left the problem to come to a final conclusion before becoming involved. When he arrived in Ahmedabad, he was able to assess the mill workers' situation quickly and advised them to strike. In doing so, he reminded them never resort to violence, never to harass the blacklegs (people who continued to work rather than strike), never to depend on donations, and to remain firm no matter how long the strike might take.

HAUNTED BY PLAGUE

Also during this time, plague broke out in the village of Kochrab, where the Satyagraha Ashram was situated. The ashram people had wanted land of their own to use as they wished, and the threat of plague was enough to prompt them to relocate. In eight days, Gandhi secured and purchased a piece of land about four miles north of their existing location. He particularly liked the spot as it was close to the Sabmarmati

Central Jail. He figured it might soon house Satyagrahis, and the community was immediately moved to the new location.

Throughout the move, the strike continued, but after the first two weeks, the strikers' resolve began to fade. Gandhi saw antagonism for the blacklegs rising and worried that violence might erupt. To rekindle the strikers' spirit, Gandhi decided to fast to death, unless the workers rallied and committed to the strike. The strikers were mortified and begged Gandhi to allow them to fast instead. When he would not yield, they vowed to maintain their resolve, but Gandhi reiterated that he would not end his fast until the strike was resolved. He told them that any funds they had when the strike began were dwindling, and they must maintain their pledge and find other work to sustain them until the strike was settled.

At the same time, the Satyagraha Ashram was busy building a weaving shed, and to solve the problem of how the laborers would support themselves during the strike, Maganlal Gandhi wondered whether a group of the strikers might be employed filling the foundation for the shed with sand. The workers thought it a grand idea, and Shrimati Anasuyabhen, one of the striking workers, filled a basket with sand and carried it on her head to the assigned place. Soon, a line of workers could be seen filling baskets and carrying sand, and Gandhi wondered how the ashram would ever be able to pay them.

However, because of Gandhi's fast, the strike would not last long. Although Gandhi insisted that he fasted to rally the workers, he had touched the hearts of the mill-owners, who set about trying to find some compromise. Meetings were held at the house of Anasuyabehn, and within three days of Gandhi's fast, the strike was settled. It had lasted three weeks. But the Kheda situation had not resolved, as Gandhi thought it would. He was not able to revel in the victory at Ahmedabad long before plowing ahead toward the next task.

In Kheda, a set crop yield would command a governmental tax from the peasants. The crop failures were such that year that the entire district was close to famine. Yet, the government would not bend to the problem and insisted that farmers pay the tax. For assistance, the peasants petitioned the Gujarat Sabha, an advocacy group of which Gandhi was president. After attempts at rectifying the situation failed, Gandhi advised the landowners to institute Satyagraha and told them not to pay the tax.

During this campaign, whatever Gandhi did was recorded in the press. The wealthy from Gujarat and Bombay sent donations to help in the struggle, but Gandhi was adamant about Satyagrahis understanding the value of simplicity. To help them better understand the principles of Satyagraha, Gandhi and his coworkers marched from village to village, urging peasants to stand firm in their resolve and not to be intimidated by the government. Government was supposed to be the servant of the people, not their master. As the people began to exhibit greater courage and resolve, the government began to take coercive actions. Officials seized property, sold the farmers' cattle, and attached crops growing for the following yield. These measures upset some peasants so much that they capitulated and paid what was owed.

To teach the farmers that Satyagraha, by its nature entailed passive civil disobedience, Gandhi wanted to have a crop of onions removed from a piece of land that had been attached by the government for non-payment of the tax. It was an unlawful attachment, so it was only right that the land bear no crops at all. Gandhi knew that whoever removed the onion crop would be liable for fines or imprisonment, but that was to be the lesson. Satyagrahis needed to be prepared to suffer to attain their goals. Sergeant Mohanlal Pandya and some of his friends volunteered to remove the crop and were subsequently arrested, as expected. The farmers rallied, as Gandhi had hoped. Many of them crowded into the courtroom for Pandya and his associates' trial, while the group was convicted and sentenced to short terms of imprisonment. A stream of followers escorted the prisoners to the jail and continued to support them throughout their incarceration.

A PYRRHIC VICTORY

Yet, the Satyagraha process in Kheda came to an unsatisfactory end. Gandhi received word that the government would forgive the debts owed by only the poor farmers, while the wealthy would still have to pay the levy. The people expressed a willingness to accept the terms, but few benefited. The government had left deliberation of who was and who was not poor to the farmers, and they could not decide among themselves. Gandhi thought that the people had weakened and were unable to carry on the campaign, so he acquiesced to the government's concession. Had the people been able to exercise their rights more fully, the struggle might have been more successful. Gandhi thought that each struggle should end with the Satyagrahis gaining in both strength and spirit, whereas the Kheda struggle did not.

The campaign was successful, however, in that it raised the awareness of the people all over India. Though Home Rule advocates, led by people like Bal Gangadhar Tilak, a journalist who headed an extremist movement in Southern India for India's freedom, and Annie Besant (by then, president of the Indian National Congress), had already interested the common people, who suffered the most from oppression, Kheda raised the awareness of the higher, more educated classes.[1] Indians, regardless of life station, began to identify with one another as Indians. The idea that the people's future lay in their own hands and in their ability to withstand hardship came to the forefront.

During the Kheda campaign, World War I was still raging in Europe. Gandhi was summoned by Lord Chelmsford to be part of a war conference that would be held in Delhi. Although Gandhi objected that other Indian independence leaders, such as the Ali Brothers, could not attend because of their incarceration.[2] Gandhi sought goodwill with the Muslims, knowing they were significant in the Indian push for fair treatment and never hesitated to promote their cause along with his own. Because of his openness toward Muslims, Gandhi had spoken at the Muslim League in Calcutta and had begun correspondence with the government regarding the Ali Brothers' release.

> It would be a wonderful act on the part of the Government if, without the knowledge of anybody, an order was sent for their discharge. Such a manner of discharging them would avoid all delirious demonstration that would otherwise inevitably take place to receive them.[3]

Gandhi agreed to attend the conference, but many of his compatriots were not happy with the decision. However, he supported a resolution on recruiting, speaking Hindustani, and won back the hearts of his countrymen. It was the first time the majority language of the people of India had been spoken at any Viceregal conference. This stunned Gandhi. The very idea that the country's prominent language should be applauded at a conference regarding that country was unthinkable.

Gandhi promised the Viceroy that he would find recruits for the army and that he would support the war, as he was still in support of the Crown. In the same letter to the Viceroy, he also stated, "I write this, because I love the English Nation, and I wish to evoke in every Indian the loyalty of the Englishman."[4]

To fulfill his promise, Gandhi returned to Kheda, in the midst of the struggle, which was still unsettled. He and his fellow recruiters had to make the long journey from village to village on foot. That meant walking about twenty miles each day, carrying enough food to sustain them throughout the march. The party held meetings in every town, but an average of one or two men signed up in each place.

HEALTH ISSUES

The recruiting had an adversely affected Gandhi's health. He had lived on groundnut butter, made from roasted nuts (akin to peanut butter), and lemons during that time and ate too much butter, which gave him a bout with dysentery, but he insisted on continuing his rounds. In the town of Nadiad, great pain beset Gandhi, but he would not accept any medication. He became feverish, restless, and worried that he might die. He asked to be taken back to the ashram. Though he would continue to suffer, the onus of recruiting was lifted, as World War I ended shortly after his return home.

Gandhi's illness was protracted to the point where he lingered near death. He obstinately refused milk and other remedies offered, and until he found his will to live overruled his own dietary restrictions, he suffered great pain from fissures, which had formed in his intestines. Finally, he agreed to drink goat's milk, and soon after, as his strength rapidly recovered, an operation was performed to repair his intestines, and he gradually recovered.

While he was still ailing, the Rowlatt Committee issued a report on the Indian situation. The committee was organized to study the "terrorist" issue in India, which had become a concern for the British Raj (rule). Home Rule groups were stirring the people, and some soldiers had been forcibly impressed. The Indian people were unhappy with the treatment they had received from the British throughout their hold over India, and after World War I, things began to get out of British control. Based on the Rowlatt committee's recommendations, legislation was passed, giving the British full authority to squelch so-called terrorists wherever their demonstrations popped up.

In his article, "From assaye to the assaye: Reflections on British government, force, and moral authority in India," historian D. George Boyce, wrote:

> The Rowlatt Report of 1918, on which was based the Anarchical and Military Crimes Act of 1919, conceded that the powers of the Defence [sic] of India Act must be reserved to the state in perpetuity, and these powers included the abandonment of trial by jury; giving powers to control movements and activities of suspects; and giving powers to detain suspects without trial and to search without warrant. This act, however, was in the tradition of earlier acts giving special powers to the authorities. They all bore testament to the fear that British rule in India was likely to collapse into anarchy if special legislation were not prepared to meet the crisis.[5]

Gandhi was livid over the proposed legislation and knew that prompt action was in order.

On February 24 1919, when he was healthy enough to travel to Ahmedabad, Gandhi had already drafted what he termed a "Pledge of Resistance." It read:

> Being conscientiously of opinion that the Bills known as the Indian Criminal Law (Amendment) Bill No. I of 1919 and the Criminal Law (Emergency Powers) Bill No. II of 1919 are unjust, subversive of the principle of liberty and justice, and destructive of the elementary rights of individuals on which the safety of the community as a whole and the State itself is based, we solemnly affirm that, in the event of these Bills becoming law and until they are withdrawn, we shall refuse civilly to obey these laws and such other laws as a Committee to be hereafter appointed may think fit and we further affirm that in this struggle we will faithfully follow truth and refrain from violence to life, person or property.[6]

Gandhi and four of his close associates signed the pledge.

However, Gandhi thought that no existing institution would endorse and sign the pledge, and therefore, he insisted that a new organization, the Satyagraha Sabha (meaning "meeting"), be established. As its principal members were from Bombay, that city was home to its headquarters, and Gandhi was its president. Yet, Gandhi's insistence on the use of Gujarati as its language and his emphasis on truth and ahimsa (nonviolence) caused dissention among the members. Although he saw the organization doomed to a short life, he and the members dove into the work at hand, and soon, the pledge was being circulated and signed by significant numbers.

HARTAL AND VIOLENCE

Gandhi's initial proposal was to call a general strike by all Indian workers. He wanted to halt business for one day and for each worker to assume a twenty-four-hour fast. This *hartal*, which is Gujarati for a day of mourning or protest, was quickly embraced and fixed to occur on March 30, 1919. The date was subsequently changed to April 6.

News of the *hartal's* date change did not reach Delhi in time, and Hindus and Muslims in the capital gathered on March 30, with the express purpose of demonstrating against the Rowlatt Act. This uncommon unity between religious factions unnerved British officials. As long as the two sides were apart, they could be controlled, but if they united, there was no telling how hard it would be to keep them in their place. This unease led to violence. As a procession of marchers neared the railway station, troops opened fire on the crowd, and there were many casualties.

News of the melee in Delhi did not spread throughout the country immediately. Mass media, such as television or the Internet, was not available to carry the news. Without knowledge of the events, thousands came to join the hartal on April 6 in Bombay, and Gandhi marched with the crowd to Chowpati, where everyone bathed in the Arabian Sea. Women and children were among the crowd, comprising of a variety of indigenous religious groups. The fast and march in Bombay were an overwhelming success.

During this gathering, Gandhi used the time to anticipate acts of civil disobedience. The long-abhorred tax on salt became a focus for Gandhi, partly because a powerful element had already been agitating for its repeal. Gandhi suggested that the people might prepare their own salt, using saltwater from the sea. Another of Gandhi's proposed tactics was to sell seditious literature. *Hind Swaraj* and Gandhi's translation of *Unto this Last* were the first items to be printed and sold openly, and the action's implementation was speeded by the *hartal*, via which many copies were sold. Proceeds were to aid with the civil disobedience campaign. However, the projected and welcomed by-product of the sale did not follow. No one was arrested. The government's stance was that Gandhi's books had never been banned.

On April 8, after finally hearing news of the events in Delhi, Gandhi set out by train to assess the situation but at the last stop was advised that he was barred from the Punjab province. Officials worried that Gandhi's appearance might cause rioting, and when Gandhi reached Palwal, at the Punjab border, he prepared to be arrested. He told the coworker with him to continue his journey to Delhi and to tell the people in Delhi what had happened. As Gandhi had anticipated, he was taken from the train and into police custody. Gandhi was politely asked to leave the area, but he refused. The police then took him back to Bombay and released him.

The news of Gandhi's arrest had infuriated crowds all over India, and arson and rioting spread throughout the country. On April 10, British soldiers arrested and deported two Congressmen in Amritsar. The people protested violently at the town hall and the post office, and on April 11, Brigadier-General Reginald Dyer moved in to take over security for the town. One of his first acts was to issue an order prohibiting public gatherings, although it was issued in English, which many inhabitants did not understand. There was no attempt to get the information to the public for whom it had been intended. Not in defiance of the regulation, but in ignorance of it, Hindus and Muslims gathered in the city on April 13, to celebrate the Sikh religious holiday of Baisakhi, which celebrates brotherhood in the community. Hearing of the intended gathering, Dyer sent his troops to the public square known as Jallianwala Bagh, where more than 10,000 people had gathered. As a speaker was talking to the crowd, Dyer appeared with about fifty armed soldiers, and without first ordering the crowd to disburse, he ordered his troops to fire on the unarmed crowd. Nearly four hundred people were killed and more than 1,500 casualties occurred from the shooting, which continued for ten minutes. Not many were able to escape the massacre, as the other three sides of the square were enclosed by buildings.

Under orders from Dyer, the injured were left unassisted for seventy-two hours, and martial law was ordered throughout the Punjab. Many Indians were flogged for not succumbing to British authority. Stories of seizure, beating and torture, and even bombing were rampant, and an order was issued prohibiting the information from being leaked outside the territory.

REVERSAL OF A GANDHI DECISION

On the afternoon of the massacre, Gandhi was in Ahmedabad, urging that Indians protest violently. Gandhi feared that by instituting Satyagraha, he had incited people to an action they did not understand. To most Indians, strikes included violence by nature. Until he could repair the situation, Gandhi suspended Satyagraha when he returned to Bombay on April 18. Many of Gandhi's former supporters were outraged and chastised him for abandoning the campaign. Gandhi knew that he had to recruit a troop of volunteers to teach the principles of Satyagraha to the people before the program could resume.

In August, events in the Punjab were finally leaked to the rest of India. Hearing of the persecution and death there, Gandhi felt responsible. The news only strengthened his belief in the need to teach the principles of Satyagraha to the people. To help in this effort, Gandhi was given control of two newspapers—*Young India*, an English-language weekly, and *Navajivan*, a Gujarati monthly. Publication of both was shifted to the Satyagraha Ashram, just as with the *Indian Opinion* in South Africa. Self-publication would avoid censorship by the government, which might occur if he used commercial printers.

There would be much to print. The shameful occurrences in the Punjab had created deep animosity. The British were not about to relinquish control; Indians wanted their country back. However, the British realized that some concessions were necessary. In the Punjab, hundreds of people who had been held without trial were released. And the Rowlatt Act, although not repealed, was not enforced. British Lords Montagu and Chelmsford drew up a bill of reforms, embodied in the *Government of India Act of 1919*. The law would restructure the Indian government as a diarchy, or a government ruled by two powers. The Indian Assembly would sit in Delhi and the body would be elected by the people. The true power would remain with the Viceroy and his council. Most department heads would be Indian, but they would be elected by property owners, who made up only 2.8 percent of the total population. A session of the Indian National Congress was called to discuss the proposition.

Gandhi arrived in Amritsar, where the conference was held, with an eye toward compromise. Although he condemned British actions in the Punjab, he saw what had happened as indicative of human nature. To Gandhi, both sides were wrong. Not long after his arrival at Amritsar, Gandhi was told that Congressional sentiment was against him, and he considered leaving town without attending the conference at all, but his friends would not let him. At the meeting of 7,031 delegates, Gandhi sat on the dais, wearing his traditional Indian dress and a brimless hat made from homespun cotton, popularized as the Gandhi cap. The cap later became the symbol for nationalism and people often saluted anyone wearing one.

Gandhi was pleased to find that many in the audience were for him, as he could tell by their chanting of his name. Motilal Nehru presided over the meeting. He was the father of Jaharwalal Nehru, an ardent Gandhi follower. Motilal knew that it would not be a wise move to stand staunchly against the Montagu-Chelmsford Act, when Gandhi had expressed views in favor of the compromise. Although he was also against the proposal, Tilak was the first to recommend its approval, as a way to prove to everyone that it would not work. Other members of the Congress agreed that this might be the best way to tackle the situation, and the Congress pledged to accept the diarchy as a step toward complete parliamentary government.

Gandhi was still alarmed about the dissention between Hindus and Muslims. He saw that each religion was completely different, not only in faith, but in culture and style. He recognized that it would be difficult to get the people of both sects thinking in the same direction, while allowing each to maintain their own identity. Gandhi's earnestness in this matter was evidenced by his defense of the Ali brothers. Partly due to his efforts, the brothers were released from prison in time to attend the

Amritsar conference. Gandhi had also addressed many Muslim gatherings and was invited to a Delhi conference on the Khalifat in October 1919.

When the Treaty of Versailles was signed, the fate of Turkey, as an axis and thereby defeated combatant, was uncertain. The Sultan of Turkey was Caliph, head of the Muslim religion, and protecting the routes to the Muslim holy city of Mecca was his chief responsibility. Muslims thought that the allied powers were preparing to cut off this route, eliminate the Sultan, and put their own puppet into power. As Hindus were the majority religion in India, Muslims saw the need to make Hindus their allies in fighting this decision. The Khalifat conference in Delhi was chiefly a protest and a show of solidarity, arranged by Muhammad Ali Jinnah, another English-educated lawyer and important Muslim leader.

THE KHILAFAT CONFERENCE

On November 24, the conference opened with Gandhi presiding. He saw the proposed restructuring of territories as a blow to Muslim faith. The Muslims were so anxious to gain Hindu support that they offered to halt all cattle slaughter, as Hindus consider cows sacred. Gandhi thought this was going too far, and spoke his mind about the issue. "If their cause was right, it was right and [they were] not going to soil it by driving bargains."[7] Yet, they could do little to prevent something that had not yet been settled.

During this discussion, Gandhi had a momentous idea. It was not a new idea, but one that had worked in the past. Rather than *hartal,* they considered launching a policy of complete non-violent, non-cooperation with the government should the decision go against them. He wanted people to quit civil service jobs, renounce titles, and show complete disregard for the government in place. Yet, the Muslims were not enthusiastic about his proposal, and the discussion ended.

After the conference, Gandhi continued to support Muslims and to debate policy with Muslim leaders. As he saw it, Muslims had only two options, because they would not be able to begin a war with England when they had no armaments. The only alternatives were migration to a Muslim country or institution of the policy of non-cooperation he had suggested.

On April 28, 1920, Gandhi became president of the Home Rule League, which had been started by Annie Besant. In early 1915, she had launched tirades in her two papers—*New India* and *Commonweal,* demanding self-governance for India. Her views coincided with those of Tilak, who in April 1916 founded a Home Rule League at the Bombay

Provincial Conference. Later that year, Annie Besant established a Home Rule League of her own. Each League would have its own sphere of influence with Tilak's in Maharashtra and Besant's everywhere else. The main purpose of both was to promote political awareness and to build up agitation for home rule. Many moderate Congressmen now joined the Home Rule Leagues as an alternative to Congressional inactivity regarding the issue.

Besant and Gandhi had parted ways in February 1916 when he had addressed the inauguration attendees at Benares Hindu University, where Besant also spoke. Gandhi criticized the bejeweled maharajas (princes) in the audience, and said, "There is no salvation for India unless you strip yourselves of this jewelry and hold it in trust for your countrymen."[8] Besant could no longer abide Gandhi's comments when he stated that to die for Indian independence would be an honorable death she told him to "Stop it!"[9] When the audience encouraged Gandhi to continue, Besant and the decorated princes left the dais, putting an end to his pro-*Swaraj* (pro-freedom) speech.

Besant was arrested during the summer of 1917 and charged with sedition, which made her a national hero and the reason for a nationwide protest. Many stayed away from Congress until this time; even Gandhi was not a member, until his election as Home Rule League president in 1920. Neither Besant nor Muhammad Jinnah agreed with Gandhi's policies at the time, and both, who had been Home Rule League prime leaders, resigned their memberships when he changed the name of the group to *Swarajya Sabha* (*Swarej* Society).

Personal issues also beleaguered Gandhi in 1920. He fell in love with a Danish blonde, blue-eyed beauty named Esther Faering. She fell in love with Gandhi's spirituality and his commitment to help others. It is uncertain what type of relationship they had. Gandhi, who had taken the brahmacharya (celibacy) vow, may or may not have been true to it. However, Gandhi did show signs of the jealous lover when it came to Faering. He once wrote to her to chastise her for going to a wedding without him or his permission. "I am filled with anxiety about you. I know it is stupid to be anxious. God is above us all."[10] Eventually, she left the ashram and returned to Denmark to care for her aging father. When Gandhi found out she had become engaged to a doctor, he went into seclusion to fast and pray for two weeks.

By the summer of 1920, it became apparent that what was still remaining of the Ottoman Empire would be divided, as the Muslims had suspected it would be, and when the Treaty of Sevres was signed on August 10, depriving Muslims of control of their holy places, Indian Muslims became angered, along with Muslims throughout the world. On June 22, 1920, Gandhi wrote to the Viceroy, "It is, then, because I believe in the British Constitution that I have advised my Mussulman [Muslim] friends to withdraw their support from Your Excellency's Government, and the Hindus to join them, should the Peace Terms not be revised in accordance with solemn pledges of Ministers and the Muslim sentiment."[11] On June 9, the Khalifat Committee had already agreed unanimously to proceed with Gandhi's non-cooperation plan and set the date for the movement to begin for August 1.

LOSS OF A GREAT LEADER

On that day, Gandhi received word that Tilak had died during the night. He was grieved by the great leader's passing, but Gandhi was in position to fully assume leadership in the fight for home rule in India. He encouraged lawyers to renounce the bar and to settle court cases among their clients via arbitration. He also recommended that students leave government-sponsored schools to attend Indian schools. Gandhi himself returned medals he had been given for his work in South Africa and encouraged Indians to boycott the forthcoming elections held under the Government of India Act of 1919.

In late November, early December 1920, when the elections were held, voter turnout was very light. Some of the candidates, adhering to the governmental boycott, had already resigned from the ballot. In December, when the Indian National Congress held its annual meeting at Nagpur, Gandhi's resolution for non-cooperation was accepted. The plan was formally expanded to include not only the surrender of titles and honors awarded by the British government, the boycott of government schools, and the abandonment of the European court system, but a boycott of foreign clothing, resignation from government service, and encouragement of non-violent civil disobedience, including non-payment of taxes.

This formal acceptance of the non-violent movement by Congress gave it increased vigor, and by January 1921, the plan was in full swing. Gandhi and the Ali Brothers toured the country, speaking to Indians about the movement. Thousands of students left schools and colleges and re-matriculated at the more than 800 Indian schools that arose nearly overnight. Many leading lawyers left their practices. Yet, the most successful and boycott-accessible to the entire population was the shunning of foreign cloth. Volunteers went from home to home collecting anything made of cloth that was not spun in India and each community held a bonfire to destroy the foreign goods. The value of foreign imports plummeted. Khadi, cotton material made from Indian homespun thread, became the uniform of the movement. Another dramatic move was to boycott the Prince of Wales when he came to visit India in November 1921. A day of *hartal* was observed the moment he landed, and rather than find adoring crowds, cheering his arrival, Prince Edward found closed shutters and empty streets. As the people's actions became more outrageous to the British, the movement strengthened in power and the Muslim-Hindu alliance also grew in strength. However, the tender alliance was not to last.

In July 1921, at the All India Khalifat Conference in Karachi, Muhammad Ali declared that it was no longer lawful for Muslims to serve in the British Army and asked that his message be conveyed to every Muslim in the army at that time. His speech resulted in his arrest. Before this happened, Gandhi had been asked to persuade the Ali brothers to control their speeches, so as not to provoke violence, and although he had counseled them, the brothers never saw eye-to-eye with Gandhi. Gandhi was successful in getting the Ali brothers to write a disclaimer regarding their incendiary statements, and even though he had treated them as brothers, they would come to repudiate Gandhi and his tactics. Gandhi worried that their violent natures would blight the movement and continued to encourage a commitment to nonviolent demonstration. His fears came to fruition on February 4, 1922 at Chauri Chaura.

Gandhi had warned Viceroy Lord Reading to release the thousands of Indian prisoners then crowding the jails, to alleviate harsh restrictions, and to allow freedom of the Indian press or the demonstrations would intensify on February 11 when no taxes would be paid in the district of Bardoli, Gujarat. Fueled by Gandhi's public ultimatum to the Viceroy, severe violence in Chauri Chaura broke out when a parade of citizens marched past a police station there. Some of the marchers were harassed by policemen as they passed, which led to violence and, ultimately, the police station set ablaze. Policemen who tried to escape the flames were hacked to pieces by the angry mob. In the aftermath, Gandhi suspended all civil disobedience and assumed all responsibility for the crime. On February 12, Gandhi assumed a five-day fast to repent for the crime and wrote, "Crimes will certainly take place in this world. We are no doubt responsible for them but they are an indirect responsibility. However, there are certain crimes for which we are directly responsible. We have but to atone for those."[12]

In rescinding Satyagraha for the second time, Gandhi lost respect, not only with the young men who had aggressively followed him, but with older participants, who said he had become irresponsible. Gandhi also thought he had disgraced himself. This gave the Viceroy an opening, as the British noticed that Gandhi was much weaker. One month after Chauri Chaura, Gandhi was arrested and sentenced to a jail term of six years. During Gandhi's incarceration, he became thoroughly introspective. He spun cotton thread on his wheel or *charka*, which he turned hour after hour, meditating on the past events of his life and the future of India. He took vows of silence and solitude for weeks at a time, during which he silently sat spinning, without visitors and with little food.

Yet, fasting wore on Gandhi's physical constitution. He dropped from 114 to under ninety-nine pounds, and his body trembled uncontrollably. When the prison doctor finally examined Gandhi, he was found to be suffering from appendicitis, although the infection was not yet acute. He continued to suffer for six months before allowing a doctor to perform an appendectomy. After the operation, Gandhi was released from prison in acknowledgment of his declining health. In early March, he went to live in Juhu beach at the home of a friend. Owing to Gandhi's penchant for nursing, he invited others to become his housemates. All had illnesses to which he could minister. He spent his days nursing, spinning, and regaining his strength, with no apparent need to get back into the political fray.

CALLED TO THE FOREFRONT

Muhammad Ali, who was at the time presiding over the Indian National Congress, pled with Gandhi to reassume the presidency the following year, but Gandhi shunned the invitation, until Motilal Nehru pledged his party's full support to Gandhi. Eventually, all of the great leaders of India were pleading with him to come back. Gandhi finally agreed to take on the presidency, but only if every member of Congress wore clothing made from Khadi and promised to spin at least 2,000 yards each, per month.

In mid-September 1924, Gandhi moved to the home of Muhammad Ali, as he prepared to retake the leadership of Indian nationalism. Two days later, Gandhi received word that a riot had broken out in Kohat, where more than one hundred people were dead or mortally injured. To atone for the latest violence in the country, Gandhi pledged a twenty-one day fast, which he barely survived.

When he had sufficiently recovered, he roamed throughout India in 1925. He had placed tremendous importance on spinning. It became a symbol of Indian unity and worked toward decline in the British economy. Gandhi thought that spinning yarn was the most important thing an

Indian could do for the cause and maintained his requirement of 2,000 yards per month for his party members. He insisted that if they were unable to do it, they should pay someone else to do it. To Gandhi, spinning was important to winning their freedom.

NOTES

1. Tilak is known by Indians as the father of Indian unrest. He often fought the moderate measures of Gokhale, leading to his split from the Indian National Congress in 1907. His motto, "Swaraj is our birthright," was the mantra of freedom fighters in India, long before Gandhi returned from South Africa.

2. Muhammad and Shawkat Ali were prominent Muslims who promoted Indian self-rule and were imprisoned for preaching anti-British resistance.

3. M.K. Gandhi, "Letter to Private Secretary to Viceroy," March 25, 1918, *Collected Works of Mahatma Gandhi Online*, Vol. 16, p. 359. http://www.gandhiserve.org/cwmg/VOL016.PDF.

4. M.K. Gandhi, "Letter to Viceroy," April 29, 1918, *The Collected Works of Mahatma Gandhi Online*, Vol. 17, p. 10. http://www.gandhiserve.org/cwmg/VOL017.PDF.

5. D. George Boyce, "From Assaye to the Assaye to the Assaye: Reflections on British Government, Force, and Moral Authority in India," *The Journal of Military History* 63, No. 3 (July 1999), pp. 643–68.

6. Gandhi, "The *Satyagraha* Pledge," February 24, 1919, *The Collected Works of Mahatma Gandhi Online*, Vol. 17, p. 297.

7. Ashe, *Gandhi*, p. 202.

8. Quoted in Wolpert, *Gandhi's Passions*, p. 86.

9. Quoted in Wolpert, *Gandhi's Passions*, p. 86.

10. Quoted in Wolpert, *Gandhi's Passions*, p. 105.

11. M.K. Gandhi, "Letter to Viceroy," June 22, 1920, *The Collected Works of Mahatma Gandhi Online*, Vol. 20, p. 415. http://www.gandhiserve.org/cwmg/VOL020.PDF.

12. M.K. Gandhi, "Letter to Chaganlal Gandhi," February 12, 1922, *The Collected Works of Mahatma Gandhi Online*, Vol. 26, p. 159. http://www.gandhiserve.org/cwmg/VOL026.PDF.

Chapter 10

A FREE INDIA AND AN UNHOLY DEATH

At the end of 1925, the conservative Tory party took power in England again. Stanley Baldwin became its Prime Minister and Lord Irwin came to Calcutta as India's new Viceroy. In early 1927, Lord Birkenhead, the ultra-conservative Secretary of State for India, organized a committee, later called the Simon Commission, after its leader, Sir John Simon, to derive the next reforms for India; however, not one Indian was invited on the panel. All Indian organizations planned to boycott the hearings, but Gandhi's personal position was to withdraw. He had turned over his Congressional presidency in December 1925 and, with the new turn of events, decided to take a year off to concentrate on writing, spinning, and the needs of those living at his ashram. Public life had become too arduous.

The ashram welcomed a new member in 1926—Madeleine Slade, whom Gandhi would rename Mirabehn.[1] She was the daughter of British Admiral Slade and had been introduced to Gandhi by her friend Romain Rolland, who won the Nobel Prize for Literature in 1915 for *Jean-Christophe*. He would later become a Gandhi biographer, referring to Gandhi as "another Christ."[2] Mirabehn would remain one of Gandhi's closest disciples until the end of his life.

The beginning of 1926 brought new life to the ashram, but the end of the year was marked by a loss. On December 23, 1926, Swami Shraddhanand, a devotee of Gandhi's who had worked for the poor and organized meeting and marches for home rule, was assassinated. He was killed by a Muslim, who was unhappy with his stand on Muslim–Hindu unity. In the wake of Shraddhanand's death, Gandhi's blood pressure rose to an alarming rate and his doctor prescribed complete rest. Gandhi may have suffered a mild heart attack. No other treatment aside from bed rest was advised.

To recuperate in a cooler climate and to finish writing his autobiography, Gandhi stayed secluded in a friend's home in Bangalore at the end of April 1927. Yet, Gandhi was continually criticized, and in the same year, for not rushing to his home territory's aid, when Gujarat was devastated by terrible floods. Gandhi ignored the remarks. He was still recuperating from his illness and thought that his time was better spent in ministering to all of India.

The most vexing of problems that year was the near complete breakdown in Hindu–Muslim relations. In September 1927, Muhammad Jinnah organized a conference at Simla, hoping to regain the brotherhood once found in a productive conference in Lucknow, 11 years before. However, Gandhi thought that Jinnah's conference and one held by the Indian National Congress in late October were pointless and did not attend either.

By the end of November, he was invited to speak with the Viceroy himself in Delhi, although they could not relate to one another. Irwin thought Gandhi a country bumpkin with no basis in reality, owing to Gandhi's attachment to the spinning wheel, whereas Gandhi thought that Irwin was "a good man with no power."[3] Each had misconceptions, and not much was accomplished by the meeting.

Gandhi's concern had to remain with his declining health. He had convinced himself that every health issue was the result of transgression and that he was in a state of self-imposed atonement. His interest in the Congress continued to wane, as he thought it bore no resemblance to the body for which he had drafted a constitution only a few years before.

TROUBLE WITH NEHRU

Gandhi was also at odds with Jaharwalal Nehru, who had become increasingly militant. At the Madras conference, the first resolution brought was the young Nehru's, and it included not only a provision for Indian self-rule, but also control of the Indian army. Gandhi was shocked by his flamboyance, whereas Nehru considered Gandhi's ideals and methods archaic. But Nehru did not understand the enormity of Gandhi's plan. Gandhi did not simply want to free India; he wanted to convert the world to his ideals. He intended that the British join his way and that India would not need to be freed because the English would become peaceful allies in a better world. He wrote in a *Young India* newspaper article, "Through the deliverance of India, I seek to deliver the so-called weaker races of the earth from the crushing heels of Western exploitation in which England is the greatest partner."[4] Gandhi also encouraged Nehru to break free of him and to pursue his own ideals.

Meanwhile, Gandhi's health continued to be an issue. His blood pressure rose so high again that he was confined to the ashram, and he kept reclining as much as possible. He was unable to attend the All-Parties Conference in Delhi, held to protest the Simon Commission, to which no Indian delegates had been invited, although a new Indian constitution had been drafted. Jaharwalal Nehru visited Gandhi to obtain his advice regarding an Indian response to proposed constitution, but Gandhi told Jaharwalal that India was not yet prepared to draw up a constitution herself. Gandhi said that Indians should first agree to come together as a nation, but if there was to be a constitution, the agreement should include a total ban on non-Indian cloth. Motilal Nehru also consulted Gandhi on the matter, hoping to bring him back into politics. They knew he commanded the strongest following of all other people in India, and only with Gandhi's leadership could they win the struggle to control their own land.

Gandhi's acceptance of his indispensability proved to be healthy for him. After being cajoled back into the struggle, his physical constitution continued to improve until he was in the best physical condition in seven years. His first order was to get everyone reinvolved in the cause by organizing committees to collect goods made from foreign cloth and to take orders for hand-woven cloth to replace what they had lost.

In May, another boon to the movement occurred: The Labor Party, which was more liberal regarding India, came back into power, with Ramsay MacDonald as its prime minister. Owing to MacDonald's friendship with Jinnah, prospects for the next Indian National Congress seemed bright. However, MacDonald was a new leader and unsure of his position. Although he leaned toward India, he was aware of the old guard in England. Even on Jinnah's advice, he would not discard the provisions of the Simon Commission and offer India dominion status, making it a self-governing nation within the British Empire. Instead, MacDonald scheduled a series of Round Table Conferences to discuss India's readiness for freedom. In doing this, he continued to uphold the vague stance of his predecessors that was doing more to encourage India to demand total independence. In the previous year's Congress, even Gandhi had given an ultimatum of dominion status within one year or Satyagraha.

During the summer of 1929, Gandhi visited the Nehru family once again. Gandhi had been asked to head Congress that winter, but he knew that was not a good idea. Motilal was pushing his son Jaharwalal to accept the onus, and Gandhi agreed. In his next article in *Young India*, he persuaded his constituents that he was not the logical choice for president, because of his age and potential health problems. He encouraged the young Nehru's election, which suited his purpose. Gandhi was able to lead, with or without the honor; Jaharwalal thought he had been given a second-hand nod.

In August, Gandhi traveled to Bombay to meet with Jinnah; however, with the uncertainty of British actions, their meeting could be little more than polite conversation. They both agreed that India needed to find its nationalism, rather than the religious sectarianism that was pulling the country apart from within. Yet, no plans for moving forward on any front could be drawn.

Soon after this meeting, Gandhi fell ill again with dysentery, caused by a diet of only raw vegetables and grains. He was forced to his bed at the ashram and reverted to a diet of goat's milk, fresh fruit juice, and diluted curds, rather like cottage cheese.

"PURNA SWARAJ!"

At the outset of the 1930 Congress, with dominion status still not granted to India or any progress toward that end, delegates and the new president of Congress, Jaharwalal Nehru, prepared for Satyagraha, fully intending to win autonomy. The battle cry would be "*Purna Swaraj!*" meaning "Complete Independence!" The entire nation took a pledge on January 26, 1930, to win independence or to die trying. The day would forever be known as *Purna Swaraj* Day. In the draft of the people's pledge, Gandhi stated that India had been ruined economically, politically, culturally, and spiritually, and wrote, "We hold it to be a crime against men and God to submit any longer to a rule that has caused this fourfold disaster to our country."[5] A few days later, Gandhi also published a list of reforms that were required, if England was to avoid nationalist civil disobedience. Included in the list were reduction of military expenditures by 50 percent, levy of a protective tariff on foreign cloth, discharge of all political prisoners who were not accused or convicted of murder, and abolition of the salt tax.

As human bodies need the mineral to survive, salt will always be a valuable commodity, but in 1930, Indian law prevented collection of natural salt, and trafficking in salt bore these consequences: "Contraband salt means salt or salt earth [natural salt] which has not paid duty. 1. Manufacture, removal, or transport of salt without licence [sic]; 2. The excavation, collection, or removal of natural salt or salt earth; 3. And possession or sale of contraband salt are [sic] punishable with a fine up to Rs. 500 [500 rupees] or imprisonment up to six months or both."[6]

On March 2, Gandhi wrote once again to Lord Irwin and advised him that, on March 11, he would join members of his ashram in practicing civil disobedience concerning the salt laws. Irwin only replied that Gandhi's decision was regrettable. When Gandhi and his followers left the ashram to begin the march, he told them they would not return until India was free. They left at 6:30 A.M. and stopped at Chandola, seven miles away, where Gandhi told ashram women and children to turn back and do their part in their homes. At his second stop, he found people who continued to wear foreign clothing and was disappointed. He told them to discard foreign luxuries and that only homespun cloth would bring them freedom.

Gandhi continued his journey, expecting to be arrested each day, yet no one ever came to arrest him. During the march, Gandhi encouraged students to leave their schools and join the fight for freedom. He also taunted the government, saying that he had already made seditious speeches and was on his way to break the law. Still, no one came to arrest him, and he asked the people how they could be afraid of such a government.

On April 5, the marchers reached Dandi, on the southeastern coast of Gujarat. At 61 years old, Gandhi and his followers had walked 241 miles in 24 days. The next morning, he marched to the sea and picked up a lump of salt that had dried on the sand. Some 2,000 people looked on and many followed Gandhi's example. On April 7, several marchers were arrested in the village of Aat, where police forcibly tried to take the salt from them. One man's wrist was broken, causing villagers of every age to dig for salt of their own to hold.

Each day, the people picketed the salt factory, and each day, Gandhi expected to be arrested. His sons Ramdas and Devdas were arrested on April 10. Then, hundreds of women emerged from their protected cocoons as wives and daughters to picket sellers of foreign cloth in Delhi and Dandi. Gandhi also encouraged women to picket the English liquor stores in Bombay, because Gandhi saw liquor as the root of evil behavior. Near mid-month, skirmishes broke out in Calcutta, Karachi, and Gujarat when police tried to grab salt from Indian fists. Yet, this time, Gandhi remained steadfast. Satyagraha would not be rescinded again. He had motivated a nation of people who willingly participated to gain their own freedom. He would continue to stand in front of and behind them. Yet, his arrest still did not come.

THE LONG-AWAITED ARREST

On April 24, even Gandhi's personal secretary was arrested, and Gandhi was increasingly frustrated by the government's "protective" attitude toward him. He encouraged people to take as much salt as they could from the salt beds and told them that if they had a finger broken by the police to offer their wrist and then their arm. He also encouraged them not only to remove clothing made with Western fabric, but to make bonfires and burn it all and to wear only Khadi. He told the men that they needed no more than the simple loincloth that he had adopted for daily wear. (He also used a Khadi shawl for warmth, when needed.) After all his seditious talk and disobedience to civil authority, just past midnight on May 5, 1930, a British magistrate and a troop of police officers finally came to arrest Gandhi.

News of Gandhi's arrest spread throughout the country quickly, and people poured into the streets to protest, until they were taken to jail themselves. Before the year ended, 60,000 Satyagrahis would be arrested and jailed, causing every cell in India to be full. From his own cell, Gandhi tried to convince Viceroy Irwin that the 300 million people of India would no longer be held hostage. Yet, words alone would not suffice. The violence of the nonviolent movement would intensify.

On Mary 21, 1930, Gandhi's son Manilal and Sarojini Naidu led a crowd of protestors to the gates of the salt plant in Dharasana, which was protected by an army of armed and helmeted police. As each line of marchers approached, they were beaten, one by one, until all of the men fell. Not one of them raised an arm to protect himself. In only a few minutes, broken, bleeding bodies lay in a heap at the gate and the men just kept on coming. Manilal Gandhi and Naidu had been arrested, rather than beaten, but the violence continued.

The year 1930 saw the time of the Great Depression cover the globe, and the Indian revolt had made matters much worse in England. Millions of British factory workers were laid off because of the Depression, but the trouble in India exacerbated the condition in the mother country. The viceroy wanted an end to the clamor and sent former Congressmen Tej Banhadur Sapru and M.R. Jayakar as emissaries to visit Gandhi in jail. They were to ask him to join a Round Table Conference in London, on behalf of the Indian National Congress. Gandhi agreed, providing he could bring up the issue of independence. Then, he would stop civil disobedience, but picketing of the cloth and liquor stores would continue. He said that he would also put a halt to looting of the salt beds as long as Indians were permitted to obtain their salt from the sea, and he insisted that all Satyagraha prisoners be released.

On August 14, 1930, the Nehrus, Sarojini Naidu, Vallabhbhai Patel, and two other Congressional leaders were brought to the prison to consult with Gandhi. The next day, they all signed a letter to the emissaries of the viceroy, reiterating Gandhi's demands. As the viceroy did not intend to allow these demands to be met, the first Round Table Conference convened in London at year's end without any members of the Indian National Congress present.

A week before Gandhi was released from jail, on January 26, 1931, the first Round Table Congress had ended. It had been decided that India's new central government would be a federation of all Indian states, with a bicameral legislature, although the particulars of that structure had not been determined. The plan would be finalized only after consultation with the Indian National Congress and the government of British India. Some powers were reserved by the British, including those related to the military, the treasury, and the police. Other departments were to be run by elected officials, including those of health and education. The viceroy also granted unconditional amnesty to Gandhi.

LOSS OF ANOTHER GREAT LEADER

Soon after Gandhi was released, Motilal Nehru lost his battle with severe asthma and heart failure. He told Gandhi he would not see *Swaraj* come to pass but knew that independence was imminent with Gandhi's leadership.

Yet, Gandhi did not take leadership of Congress again that year. It fell to Vallabhbhai Patel, and Gandhi met with the Congress Working Committee at Anand Bhavan to help plan its next move. Although some members wanted negotiations to continue, Gandhi was leery of allowing peace to stall their fight. Police brutality continued even though the civil disobedience had been halted, and he said, "A halting peace will be dangerous and I can see no sign of real peace coming."[7] Yet, before they renewed their war against the system, Gandhi asked to meet with Viceroy Irwin, man to man, one final time, and received a reply to come to Delhi on February 17, 1931. The pair would meet several times.

After the first meeting, Gandhi was optimistic. The viceroy seemed amenable to compromise. The only decisions made were to look into certain points of contention on both sides. They agreed to meet again the next day. Gandhi sent a wire to Congress, via a friend, telling them to stop all violence, passive or otherwise, until the meetings were over.

At the end of the second meeting, Gandhi was not as hopeful. Irwin seemed more guarded. The main sticking point was a complete end to the civil-disobedience campaign, a tack that Irwin declared he could not tolerate and Gandhi just as adamantly would not abandon. The meeting ended with Gandhi promising not to renew the civil disobedience as long as the talks were in progress and with Irwin saying that he wanted to include Sapru and Jayakar in the discussions. Gandhi agreed as long as he could invite Jaharwalal Nehru and Vallabhbhai Patel as well. The talks would continue to be between the two leaders alone.

The third meeting with Irwin was delayed by a week, while Irwin consulted with superiors in London. When Irwin was prepared, the third discussion covered all the previous points made in earlier negotiations, but the talks deepened. Each opponent tried to gain ground, but neither would concede.

At the March 1 meeting, they hit an obstacle concerning picketing and boycotting. Gandhi stressed that the picketing was lawful, as long as it was nonviolent, and the evidence of police brutality quickly brought the discussion to another topic: the salt tax. Irwin claimed that he could not sanction civil disobedience and could not deplete sources of revenue by simply repealing the law. He suggested that Gandhi meet with the finance minister to discuss the issue and, with that concession, Gandhi agreed to end the boycott and met with Irwin's secretary later that evening to iron out the details. Irwin was so pleased that he thought he was gaining ground, and wrote in his report, "I joined Mr. Gandhi and Mr. Emerson at 9.30 P.M. and found that by that time Emerson had got Mr. Gandhi hitched to the point of abandonment of the boycott as a political weapon and an assurance of complete freedom for cloth merchants to do what they liked. These seem pretty substantial gains."[8]

STRIKING AN AGREEMENT WITH CONSEQUENCES

By the fifth meeting, Gandhi wanted to address the problem of seized land, which had been resold by the government. He said that the land affected by Satyagraha campaigns should be returned to the people. Irwin refused, saying that it was not within his power, but he continued to press Gandhi on the picketing issue, since he had been able to gain ground with the boycotting issue. Gandhi was just as adamant that the picketing would not cease, though he pledged it would remain orderly and peaceful. The talks ended with a provisional agreement, which was signed by both parties on March 5, 1931. The important part of the agreement included

- discontinuance of the civil disobedience movement.
- Congress's agreement to participate in the Round Table Conference.

- withdrawal of all governmental regulations meant to impede Congress.
- withdrawal of all convictions that did not pertain to violent actions.
- release of all prisoners who participated in the civil disobedience movement.

Gandhi and Irwin were elated by their accord, but parties on both sides were unhappy with the arrangement. Nehru thought that Gandhi had given away too much, and the English thought that Irwin had bowed to a "fakir" (a Hindu ascetic who sometimes performs magic or suffers physical torture to exhibit spiritual endurance). Even British Prime Minister Winston Churchill had referred to Gandhi in such demeaning terms, and Stanley Baldwin, leader of the Tory opposition, refused to attend any Round Table Conference with the person many in England were calling the "salt thief."

On March 23, Gandhi wrote to Irwin to beg for the life of Bhagat Singh, accused of killing an army officer and bombing a public meeting hall. He did so to maintain a positive popular opinion of the agreement the two countries had just signed. "It seems cruel to inflict this letter on you, but the interest of peace demands a final appeal," Gandhi wrote. Though he probably realized what he was asking was futile, Gandhi thought he was obligated to save the nation, rather than just one man. He ended his letter by writing, "Execution is an irretrievable act. If you think there is the slightest chance of error of judgment, I would urge you to suspend for further review an act that is beyond recall."[9] Yet, that very day, Singh and his cohorts were hanged, and Nehru called a general strike to protest the death of "martyrs." This was on the eve of the annual meeting of Congress at Karachi.

Upon his arrival at the Congress, Gandhi was greeted with flag-waving protestors, proclaiming, "Down with Gandhi," but he ignored the insults.[10] However, the atmosphere inside the congress hall was not that different. Many of the younger delegates were unhappy over the settlement, and they let their views be known. Congress gathering ended in an unprecedented two days and on return to Delhi, the Congress Working Committee decided that Gandhi should be the only delegate at Round Table Conferences. Viewing the Working Committee members as old-timers, many of the young men, including Nehru, were not happy with their decision.

With the Working Committee's goodwill, Gandhi traveled to Simla to meet with the new Viceroy, Lord Willingdon, who had just taken over the post from Irwin. Willingdon was not nearly as progressive as Irwin had been and far less sympathetic to Gandhi's causes. A Round Table Conference was arranged, and in late June 1931, Gandhi prepared to visit London, where he had not been in 17 years.

ADDRESSING THE ROUND TABLE CONFERENCE

When Gandhi arrived in London on September 15, the second Round Table Conference was already in session. He addressed the Federal Structure Committee on September 15, gave the audience a primer on the Indian National Congress, and explained that he was only acting on the Congress's behalf. During his time in London, Gandhi also met with silent film star Charlie Chaplin and Muslim leader, the Aga Khan. He also met with Prime Minister Ramsay MacDonald.

When the conference ended, Gandhi did not believe that it had been fruitful for India. One sticking point had been the appointment of a block of Untouchables, Sikhs, and Muslims to the proposed bicameral legislature. To Gandhi, all sects were patriots of the same country. His health also suffered in the damp, cold British autumn, and Gandhi was ready to return home.

What brought him back to India even more quickly was a telegram from Nehru, advising him of a troubling situation in the United Province (in the modern Uttar Pradesh region), in northern India. Tenants had been thrown off their land and arrested when they returned to it. He requested to take Congress-approved action but, in light of the Irwin–Gandhi truce, wanted Gandhi's endorsement. Gandhi, disenchanted by the Round Table Conference, told him to take whatever action that Congress deemed appropriate, without hesitation.

By the time Gandhi reached Bombay on December 28, Nehru had been arrested and sentenced to two years at hard labor, as had many other Congressional leaders. "Last year we faced *lathis* [a crowd-control weapon made from a bamboo stick with a blunt metal tip], but this time we must be prepared to face bullets," Gandhi told a public meeting that day.[11] And when the Working Committee met to discuss Gandhi's negative experience at the Round Table Conference, they agreed that it was time to resume Satyagraha. That night, Gandhi was also arrested.

Being jailed did not bother Gandhi, but the fact that Great Britain had announced its intention to reserve a block of delegate seats exclusively for Untouchables did. He had remarked at the Round Table Conference that he would resist this formation with his life and soon announced that he would fast until death if the plan was put into action. On August 17,

1932, Ramsay MacDonald announced that seats would be reserved in the bicameral legislature for Muslims, Sikhs, and Untouchables, and Gandhi wrote to the Prime Minister, setting the date for his fast to begin. He gave them until September 20 to change their stance or wrote that his death would be on their hands.

When the day for Gandhi's fast to begin came, B.R. Ambedkar, political leader of the Untouchables, was upset that Gandhi would consider fasting to death for the lowest caste. He met with Gandhi on September 22 to discuss the issue and insisted that the block of promised seats was the only way that Untouchables would have political representation. Ambedkar told Gandhi it was critical to their survival. Gandhi insisted that he wanted to serve "*Harijans*," a term coined by Narasinh Mehta, a Gujarat poet, which means "children of God." Gandhi and Ambedkar worked out a mutually acceptable proposal that would promise the Harijans many more seats than the Prime Minister had awarded, and that the Harijan candidates would be included in the general election as all other Indians running for office.

Meanwhile, people all over India, including Mirabehn, began to fast in sympathy with Gandhi. However, an event would cut the suffering short. The Hindu Leaders' Conference convened in Bombay on September 25 and resolved that no Hindu should be regarded as untouchable because of birth and that Untouchables would henceforth be able to use the same road, well, or public institution as other Hindus. The declaration was wired to Ramsay MacDonald, who accepted the agreement for the British government, and on September 26, Gandhi ended his fast.

THE EVER-EFFECTIVE FAST

Gandhi had found that fasting brought results, and he continued to use the tactic repeatedly. It always worked. Yet, failure often accompanied victories. In municipal elections that took place at the end of January, every Harijan on the ballot was defeated. By not allowing them special circumstances in elections, Gandhi had not helped them at all, and the community was very unhappy. Gandhi said, "I cannot help owning to you my utter stupidity."[12] This was quite an admission, especially since he had almost starved himself to death for such a blunder. Some leaders began to question his mental capacity at age 64. However, Gandhi started another newspaper—the weekly *Harijan*.

In late April, Gandhi undertook another fast, only this time, as a penance for his own shortcomings. It would last 21 days, the longest fast he had ever endeavored. It was sparked by the discovery that many of his ashram inhabitants had broken the vow of brahmacharya. Agnostic Nehru did not understand Gandhi as he became more deeply spiritual and thought that Gandhi relied too much on magic and not enough on reality. On the first day of his fast, Gandhi was released from prison. The government worried that his death in jail would ignite more violent revolt. His fast lasted the full term; Gandhi survived.

Congressional leaders then came to visit Gandhi and asked him to call off the civil disobedience campaign that was going on all over India. Gandhi tried to meet with the viceroy before agreeing to do so, but his audience was not merely denied. Willingdon warned Gandhi against further involvement in Satyagraha, realizing that Gandhi's venerated position had been weakened by his campaigning for the Harijans. Many powerful Hindus had turned against him, and the Muslims by then were drifting closer to Jinnah as their leader. When Gandhi notified Bombay's home secretary of another Satyagraha action to boycott foreign cloth and liquor, he was arrested and taken to the Sabarmati Jail. While there, he played the fasting card again because authorities would not allow him the necessary support to publish the *Harijan* from prison. On August 14, he wrote to Bombay's home secretary and expressed his intent to resume fasting two days from the date of his letter. By August 23, he was released. Gandhi's freedom would not be interrupted again for nine years.

But perhaps Gandhi had bludgeoned the government and the people with the fasting ploy too many times. He had come to be seen as an aesthetic and a social reformer, rather than as a politician. Many of his former staunch supporters no longer took him seriously, and his advancing years did much to bolster the disdain. Unaffected, Gandhi continued the path of *ahimsa* and work for the Harijans. He thought that unless the downtrodden were accepted, Indians had no right to ask for independence. They had to learn to abide each other.

Around that time, famous people came to meet and assist in Gandhi's quests. Muriel Lester, a well-known British pacifist, and Agatha Harrison, leader of London's Quaker community, joined Gandhi's tour of Bihar in March 1934, but the atmosphere had become dangerous, as many of the militant Hindu groups were vehemently opposed to equality for Untouchables. As he was getting into his car one evening, Gandhi was attacked by high-caste Hindus, who threw stones and dented his vehicle. Gandhi escaped without injury. In mid-June, a bomb was thrown at a car thought to be carrying Gandhi. These events did not dissuade Gandhi from working toward his goals.

In September 1934, Gandhi had grown so far away from what Congress was doing that he decided to resign. He thought that the Socialists, headed by Nehru, were running things and he did not find their values to be his own. Rather than society doing for the individual, he saw self-help and self-sufficiency as the only way to reach societal harmony. Gandhi poured more of his time and affection into the poor of India to teach them these ideas. In November 1934, he founded the All-India Village Industry's Association and recruited wealthy friends as backers for the project. His aim was teaching villagers to become less dependent on imported goods and taught them that homemade or homegrown was always better.

However, constant service to the betterment of others was not always best for Gandhi. The next year, his blood pressure shot up again and he was confined to bed for nearly two months. Yet, nothing kept Gandhi down very long. When Nehru, president of Congress again that year, wanted to reject the Government of India Act of 1935 in its entirety, the Working Committee was not behind him. They thought that the legislation was a step toward dominion status for India, and the offer was better than none. Gandhi was enlisted to talk to Nehru and persuade him to reconsider. Gandhi knew that the views of the Working Committee represented the will of the people more accurately, but he was unable to make Nehru see this point of view. Nehru ridiculed the 67-year-old Gandhi, saying that he was turning back time, rather than moving forward. Still, Nehru was not able to convince Congress to reject the legislation and he was not the only unhappy party. He also contributed to the unrest among Muslims.

HINDU–MUSLIM RELATIONS WORSEN

In February 1937, when Indians went to the polls, candidates backed by Congress won 716 seats, with majorities in six of the eleven British provinces of India. Nehru, who led the Congressional campaigns, reveled in the victory, saying there were only two parties left—Congress and Britain. Jinnah, who thought that the Muslims were not in tune with Congress, was furious at Nehru's remark, saying that the Muslim League represented a third party. However, haggling was brought to a full halt when England decided that British provincial governors still held the onus of safeguarding the interests of minorities and, disregarding the accord, appointed provincial governors of their own.

Nehru was furious and ready for violent reaction, but Gandhi tried to persuade him that it was better to join the government and obstruct it from within. As Congress agreed with Gandhi, Nehru had to back down. In July, the Working Committee met to discuss the formation of ministries in the six provinces where they had won majorities. Jinnah met with

Gandhi to discuss greater Muslim participation in the areas where a majority of Indian Muslims resided—the United Provinces, Bengal, and the Punjab—as they had won only 109 seats from the total 1,585. However, Gandhi told Jinnah there was nothing he could do, thus driving the wedge between the two factions even deeper. That October, Jinnah was declared Quaid-i-Azam (great leader) of the Muslims and by then was permanently presiding over the Muslim League.

Gandhi was encouraged to meet with Jinnah again, but he declined. He knew that Nehru was not in favor of the meeting and feared losing what little power he had over Nehru more than Jinnah's power over the Muslim League. Some saw this as a politically foolish move, and the lack of Congressional concern for Muslim interests would later split the Indian nation. Yet, these were only some of the problems the Indian Nation faced and Gandhi had been dealing with them again on a daily basis. In December 1937, he had another blood pressure episode and was returned to Juhu Beach until he could recover.

Hindu–Muslim riots continued throughout the United Provinces, which was the most populated and multicultural part of all India. Late in April, Gandhi agreed to meet with Jinnah again, regardless of Nehru's strong feelings against the summit. However, Jinnah exasperated Gandhi and vice versa. Nothing was accomplished. Around this time, Gandhi found himself battling mild depression.

Partly to blame for Gandhi's mood swing was a new woman in his life: Princess Rajkumari Amrit Kaur, a Christian from the state of Kapurthala. She would take the place of Mirabehn as his most trusted confidant. Mirabehn had become upset over Gandhi's new self test of the *brahmacharya* vow, which he had taken so many years before. He claimed it strengthened his resolve to sleep naked with young, nubile women surrounding him, but Mirabehn was appalled. He referred to Mirabehn's reservations as hysteria and thought that this new test of his spiritual strength was also tied in some way to Hindu–Muslim unity. If he was able to resist sexual tension, the ideal would be realized.

Kasturba was inured to her husband's tests of sexual abstinence and his attachments to other women. Though Gandhi continued to think that she was bound to obey and go along with his every desire, Kasturba carried on a life of her own, although she still had respect for Gandhi's will. She thought of him as the people's guide, and as a good Hindu wife, she knew she would always stand beside him. Only once did she show disrespect to one of his "companions," when she bullied and chastised the woman while they worked together in Kasturba's kitchen. The tension ended when Gandhi gave each a kitchen of her own.

Gandhi was 70 by this time and had begun to consider retirement from public life. He had lost Congress entirely, as it was then in the hands of Shri Subhas Bose, whose candidacy he was strongly against because of Bose's militancy and strong attraction to national socialism. To make matters worse, what Gandhi had worked toward achieving in South Africa was unraveling in a resurgence of racism there. Plus, war was once again on the horizon, as Adolf Hitler had led the Germans in an invasion of Poland. On July 23, 1939, Gandhi wrote to Hitler, urging restraint; however, Gandhi's letter went unnoticed, no doubt because Hitler would have thought of Gandhi as a subhuman. Soon after Gandhi's letter, and without consultation of the Indian people, then Viceroy Linlithgow, speaking for India, immediately declared war on the Axis powers. Due to his stance on *ahimsa* (nonviolence), Gandhi could not support either side.

Linlithgow's declaration of war for India did more than to upset Gandhi. Nehru was furious, and Bose resigned his Congressional presidency. Nehru drafted the Congress's resolution on the war, demanding that Great Britain first declare freedom and democracy for India after the war. If the British government did so, in writing, India would be behind their efforts fully. Bose formed the Forward Bloc party, openly siding with the Axis powers, which led to his arrest and subsequent escape to Afghanistan, from which he traveled to Berlin and then, Japan. Jinnah, unlike the other two leaders, pledged unconditional Muslim support to Great Britain.

WORLD WAR II: A HALT TO PROGRESS

In hope of changing Congressional sentiment, Gandhi was invited to meet with the viceroy once again. During the meeting, Gandhi realized the viceroy's great esteem for Jinnah, who had also been educated in England and always dressed like an English gentleman. Gandhi wrote a piece for the *Harijan*, hoping again to persuade Indians to see the need for Hindu–Muslim unity not only in regard to the war, but especially in their fight for Indian freedom. However, knowing there was dissention in India, the British government put everything on hold. The India Act of 1935 could be amended, only after an assessment of Indian views, once the war had ended.

This new statement was like vinegar in the already tender wounds of India. On October 22, 1939, Congress resolved to instruct all Congress Ministries to provide their resignations. Gandhi was against it, seeing the action as an excuse for the British government to draft Indians into service for the war. Yet, Nehru insisted, and Gandhi was too tired to fight him.

Jinnah took the opportunity to proclaim December 2, 1939, as a Day of Deliverance, remarking that Congress had ceased to function. Gandhi pleaded with Jinnah to reconsider, but Jinnah was on a path. He no longer wanted Indian unity; he wanted separation. In late March 1940, the Muslim League hammered out their plan for the partitioning. Their new Muslim country would be known as Pakistan, meaning "land of the pure."

The events made Gandhi's depression worse. He became so despondent that he even stopped talking. Most saw him as little more than a visionary, not at all suited for the politics in the modern world. In mid-September 1940, Congress met in Bombay and urged Gandhi to meet with them, pulling him out of his misery. They wanted him to lead civil disobedience once again. In anticipation, Gandhi met again with the viceroy, but they came to no agreement. Gandhi left the meeting knowing what to do.

Rather than take the lead, as he had in the past, he chose a successor, Vinoba Bhave. Gandhi sent Bhave to make speeches in central Indian villages, in direct disobedience of the British gag order against antiwar demonstration. On October 21, 1940, Bhave was arrested. Nehru took up where Bhave left off and was also arrested on October 31, found guilty of sedition, and sentenced to four years of hard labor. But Congressional agitation throughout the country was not the only unrest. Civil religious wars between Hindu and Muslim took lives in greater proportion.

In February 1942, Singapore, a southeast jaunt across the Bay of Bengal, fell quickly to the Japanese, and India's army of 60,000 fell with it. At that point, the British realized that getting India's support for the war was of extreme importance and therefore took action by diplomatic means. Sir Stafford Cripps, leader of the House of Commons, was enlisted by Prime Minister Winston Churchill to fly to India and offer the Indians dominion status immediately after the war if they would agree to fight, and he sought a meeting with Gandhi. The two negotiated, but the meeting was short, as the British offered dominion status; however, to please the Muslims, a clause was added that any province that did not wish to belong to the dominion could opt out. Gandhi told Cripps that there was no way Congress would accept the plan. He told Cripps that a better arrangement would be to allow Jinnah to take on the role of leader in the new dominion government, and, in this way, it might succeed.

On learning of Gandhi's advice to Cripps, Nehru was infuriated. He called for guerrilla warfare against the British to regain what was rightfully theirs and even tried to enlist the aid of the United States in attaining India's freedom. Although President Franklin D. Roosevelt sympathized with the Indians and had counseled Churchill to give India its freedom, he could not go against the United States' greatest ally, the British. Gandhi believed that civil disobedience, noncooperation, or both were in order, and he urged Nehru to quit Congress because of his militant behavior.

PLANNING THE NEW SATYAGRAHA

When the Working Committee met on August 2, 1942, Gandhi had an outline of how the civil resistance should play out, saying that every Satyagrahi needed to understand what participation entailed: a vow to live free or die. Gandhi called his campaign "Do or die!" and it later came to be known as the "Quit India!" movement. On August 8, Congress voted on Gandhi's resolution and it passed unanimously. Gandhi, along with every member of the Working Committee, was soon arrested, as were Kasturba, Mirabehn, and Mahadev Desai, Gandhi's secretary. All were taken to the Aga Khan's abandoned palace in Poona. In the aftermath, 250 railway stations were attacked, and more than 100 police stations were burned, with 30 police officers killed.

The Khan's palace jail was difficult for its prisoners. The building was old and damp and sat on a swamp, filled with malaria-carrying mosquitoes. Desai was the first to succumb to the unhealthy conditions of the place. He had been frail for years, but with his passing on August 15, Gandhi became severely depressed. He had lost an old friend, and the Satyagraha campaign had lost its component of *ahimsa*. A violent civil war had developed, fought mostly within northern India, during the later years of World War II.

As he had done so many times before, Gandhi began another fast. However, by then, the British thought of these fasts as mere political ploys. They offered to release Gandhi from prison before he began the fast, but Gandhi refused. Therefore, they sent their best doctors to minister to Gandhi, and after 10 days began to prepare for his funeral, as he had become so weak. But he survived. Kasturba would not be so lucky. Although doctors prescribed many courses of medication for his wife, Gandhi rejected all of them. Many homeopathic remedies were tried, but to no avail. On February 22, 1944, Gandhi's wife of 63 years died and was cremated on the palace grounds. Now, Gandhi would be comforted by Manu, young daughter to his nephew Jaisukhlal. She had come to live at the Sevagram ashram after her mother died in 1942.

Gandhi was released from prison on May 6, close to his seventy-fifth birthday. He weighed less than 100 pounds. By May 11, he was on a train for Juhu Beach, where he could recover.

When World War II ended, then Viceroy Waddell made a significant blunder by inviting representatives from Congress and the Muslim community into his administration. Although it was a step toward Indian independence, as only he and the commander-in-chief were the only Englishmen remaining, he did not understand the civil atmosphere at the time. Gandhi was called to another Simla conference, and he urged the Congress Working Committee to accompany him so that he could confer with them while the talks were in progress. He was anxious to be back on the political scene, pulling strings from in front and behind, claiming to be speaking only for himself, and voicing his desire to live to be 125 years old. Even so, the Simla conference had not been productive. Gandhi blamed it on the English refusing to relinquish power.

However, in Britain, India's hope for freedom was improved when Winston Churchill's regime ended. Churchill had always been anti-Gandhi, openly referring to Gandhi as a fakir. The Labour Party's Clement Attlee had assumed the role of Prime Minister, and several of Gandhi's English friends became part of the administration. Finally, in December, Britain's Labor government prepared to transfer power with nationwide elections. Jinnah proved how strong his Muslim League had become when they won all available seats in the Central Assembly. Jinnah was happy to inform his constituents that Pakistan would soon be a reality. When Great Britain sent a triumvirate of politicians to facilitate the transition, Gandhi again told them they should put Jinnah in charge, to keep India whole and to save internal struggle in the future, but again, they did not heed his warnings.

A FREE INDIA AND LOSING MAHATMA

The Working Committee met in Delhi in April 1946 and structured a transfer of power that would allow for a weak central government, with outlying provinces controlled by Hindu or Muslim blocks strongest in each region. The provinces would retain most of the power in their respective areas of influence, while provincial assemblies would remain to oversee smaller domains inside the larger blocks. Yet, in a presidential speech to Congress in early July, Nehru said that Congress would enter the new assembly completely unfettered by agreements. Jinnah took his remark as utter rejection of the Working Committee's plan and was furious. He called for direct action and bid farewell to any further congressional activity. Calcutta turned into a battlefield on August 6, 1946, and violence throughout India waxed rather than abated.

In October, Gandhi decided to walk through the streets of Bengal, prepared to become a martyr in response to the continuing mayhem. His main objective was the establishment of a Peace Committee in each town, with one Muslim and one Hindu in control. He taught people the values behind Satyagraha, but soon, Muslim leaders harangued Gandhi, telling him to leave Muslim territory and that they could take care of their own.

Viceroy Mountbatten invited Gandhi to meet with him in March 1947 and asked Gandhi how to stop the killing. Once again, Gandhi brought up the idea of a central government with Jinnah at its head, which astounded Mountbatten. At hearing of this, Nehru began to refer to Gandhi as an old fool, saying he was out of touch with reality. Gandhi's spirits, already fallen due to the murderous behavior of his compatriots, only fell into a deeper depression. He tried to hold a prayer meeting that night, but a representative of the Hindu Mahasaba or Rshtriya Swayamsevak Sangh (R.S.S.), heckled him, though the man was not arrested. Much of Gandhi's mail was negative by that time, but he continued to think that the people who criticized him loved him. He did not recognize that many of the important and influential men had lost respect for him because of his work among the Harijans.

On July 17, Pakistan was created and India won her freedom with the Indian Independence Act of 1947. The terms of the act included partitioning of India. Gandhi foresaw the misery that action would cause, but at the time, no one seemed willing to listen to the ravings of an old man. Not long the after governmental action, the sultan of Kashmir was unwilling to side with either India or Pakistan, and a bitter struggle ensued over the territory. Nehru, claiming it was his ancestral home, even though none of his relatives had lived there in more than a hundred years, was unwilling to allow the Kashmir to fall to the Muslims, and Jinnah, seeing the land as part of Pakistan, would not relinquish control either. A bloody struggle ensued and sporadically continues into the present day.

Gandhi seemed to have given up hope of quelling the violence. On August 31, as he slept, an angry Hindu mob attacked Hydari House in Calcutta, where Gandhi was staying at the time. They tossed rocks through windows, broke into the compound and pounded on the front door. The mob presented a victim of the rioting as justification, because they claimed he had been stabbed by a Muslim. The crowd broke windows and threatened to enter the building, but police arrived and quelled the situation. The next day, Gandhi embarked on another fast. He promised only to stop when the riots ended. Many politicians came to Gandhi's bedside, imploring him to stop fasting, but he would not listen. Only when the politicians agreed to do something to stop the fighting would Gandhi eat again.

Gandhi was frustrated and angered by everything he saw. Trainloads of corpses came from Pakistan, carrying Hindus, while trainloads of dead Muslims went the opposite way. He urged Hindus to stop taking revenge on the Muslims, to which Hindu fanatics derided him by calling him Muhammad Gandhi. Gandhi also became very critical of the Congress led by Nehru, telling its members to police their own people or to resign. Gandhi contracted the flu virus, but he did not stop preaching. He continued to speak out on the murderous events in a free India where civil war had become a way of life, and on January 12, 1948, he resumed fasting to the death. "It will end when I am satisfied that there is a reunion of hearts of all communities," he said.[13]

The fast did not last long. Congress agreed to transfer Pakistan's share of British-held assets, and thousands of Indians from all religions stood outside Birla House where Gandhi was staying to beg him to end the fast. His kidneys were failing. Yet, Gandhi did not stop, until an agreement was signed in Hindi and Urdu by more than 100 Hindu leaders who promised they would live like brothers with the Muslims again. On January 20, he was carried to a platform outside to speak to the crowd gathered there, but when he began to speak, a hand grenade exploded behind him. Although another had been planned to land in Gandhi's lap, a second terrorist lost his nerve, saving Gandhi's life. Only the first man was caught and taken into custody.

On January 30, 1948, Gandhi went through his normal daily routine until dinnertime when he finished his evening meal and then, with the aid of his personal assistants, walked toward the garden for another prayer meeting. As the group walked down the path, the crowd parted for them, wishing Gandhi well, until a man approached from the right and shot Gandhi, point blank, in the chest three times. Gandhi's last words were, "Hei Ra... ma! Hei Ra... !"[14] He collapsed and died at 5:17 P.M.

At dawn, Gandhi's body was dressed in a loincloth that he had made himself. He was surrounded by flowers of all colors and types, and the flag of India was draped over him. A huge throng of people turned out to pay their last respects, and after a long procession, the body was burned on a funeral pyre, according to Hindu custom.

In 1982, Sir Richard Attenborough produced and directed the film *Gandhi*, which starred Ben Kingsley in the title role. Though he did an admirable job of the depicting the important parts of Gandhi's life and death, only so much can be shown in a movie. The man was so much more complex and his experiences more abundant than one film could portray. Still, the film won eight Academy Awards, and is highly respected in the Western world, as is Gandhi himself.

Gandhi's legacy of nonviolence was the cornerstone of the civil rights and antiwar movements of the 1960s. Though his ideals could not always be upheld, they were the impetus and the standard for change in a society hoping for an answer. Is the world at that threshold once more? Can India return to the path of *ahimsa* that Gandhi championed?

Gandhi ended his life as a martyr for peace, as he no doubt wished to die. Happily, he was gone before the unrest started again between Pakistan and India, long before the threats of nuclear war arose between people who once called themselves brothers and sisters and lived together in one India. One wonders how Gandhi might have reacted to a world where peace took more than a handshake, more than goodwill toward other people—a world where peace is only secure as long as one country does not fire missiles at another. His ideal of *ahimsa*—nonviolence in all conflicts—is not a modern concept, but never one to be forgotten.

NOTES

1. *Behn* means sister.
2. Quoted in Wolpert, *Gandhi's Passions*, p. 122.
3. Quoted in Wolpert, *Gandhi's Passions*, p. 128.
4. M.K. Gandhi, "Independence vs. Swaraj," *Young India*, January 12, 1928, *The Collected Works of Mahatma Gandhi Online*, Vol. 41, p. 106. http://www.gandhiserve.org/cwmg/VOL041.PDF.
5. M.K. Gandhi, "Draft Declaration for January 26," January 10, 1930, *The Collected Works of Mahatma Gandhi Online*, Vol. 48, p. 215. http://www.gandhiserve.org/cwmg/VOL048.PDF.
6. M.K. Gandhi, "Salt Tax," *Young India*, February 27, 1930, *The Collected Works of Mahatma Gandhi Online*, Vol. 48, p. 350.
7. Quoted in Wolpert, *Gandhi's Passions*, p. 154.
8. M.K. Gandhi, "Interview with Viceroy," March 1, 1931, *The Collected Works of Mahatma Gandhi Online*, Vol. 51, p. 197. http://www.gandhiserve.org/cwmg/VOL051.PDF.
9. M.K. Gandhi, "Letter to Viceroy," March 23, 1931, *The Collected Works of Mahatma Gandhi Online*, Vol. 51, p. 290–291.
10. Quoted in Wolpert, *Gandhi's Passions*, p. 159.
11. M.K. Gandhi, "Speech at Public Meeting, Bombay," December 28, 1931, *The Collected Works of Mahatma Gandhi Online*, Vol. 54, p. 318. http://www.gandhiserve.org/cwmg/VOL054.PDF.
12. Quoted in Wolpert, *Gandhi's Passions*, p. 170.
13. Quoted in Wolpert, *Gandhi's Passions*, p. 253.
14. Quoted in Wolpert, *Gandhi's Passions*, p. 256. Gandhi's last words translate to: "Oh, God! Oh, Go . . ."

GLOSSARY

Ahimsa Doctrine of nonviolence

Ashram Spiritual community

Bhagavad Gita A sacred Hindu text consisting of a dialogue between the Hindu god Krishna and the prince Arjuna, whereby Arjuna is instructed in ethics and the nature of the supreme being

Boers Dutch farmers (and their descendants) who migrated to South Africa

Brahmacharya Vow of celibacy

Brahmin Scholarly or priestly caste

Dalits Untouchables; lowest caste in India

Dhotis Baggy trousers

Diwan Chief minister; advisor

Fakir A Hindu ascetic who sometimes performs magic or suffers physical torture to exhibit spiritual endurance

Hartal Day of mourning or protest

Karma The relationship between cause and effect of a person's behavior that determines his or her path in the life to follow

Khadi Indian woven cloth

Mahabharata Ancient Hindu epic

Maharaja A Hindu prince ranking above a raja

Raj British rule on India from 1858 to 1947

Samskaras Impressions

Sannyasi Religious mendicant who renounces everything, including caste and convention

Satya Truth

Satyagraha Policy of nonviolent resistance

Swadeshi That which is made in or belongs to one's own country
Swaraj Freedom
Tinkathia System whereby tenant farmers were required to plant one-seventh of their holdings with indigo for a fixed price
Varnas The four divisions of Hindu society, which include the Brahmins, the Kshatriya, the Vaishya, and the Sudras; often referred to as caste
Zamindar Substantial hereditary landholder

SELECTED BIBLIOGRAPHY

Arnold, David. *Gandhi, Profiles in Power*. London: Pearson Education, 2001.

Dasgupta, S.N. *Hindu Mysticism*. New York: Frederick Ungar, 1927; reprinted 1959.

Erikson, Erik H. *Gandhi's Truth: On the Origins on Militant Nonviolence*. New York: W.W. Norton, 1969.

Ghose, Aruna, managing ed. *India*. New York: DK Publishing, 2002.

Judd, Denis and Keith Surridge. *The Boer War*. New York: Palgrave MacMillan, 2003.

Pakenham, Thomas. *The Boer War*. New York: Random House, 1979.

Shirer, William L. *Gandhi: a Memoir*. New York: Simon and Shuster, 1979; reprinted New York: Washington Square Press, 1982.

Watson, Francis. *A Concise History of India*. New York: Thames and Hudson, 1979; reprinted 1987.

INTERNET SOURCES

Collected Works of Mahatma Gandhi Online, Vols. 1–98. http://www.gandhiserve.org/cwmg/cwmg.html

Desai, Mahadev H. *Day to Day with Gandhi: Secretary's Diary*, Vol. 2. http://www.forget-me.net/en/Gandhi/day2day2.txt

Gandhi, M.K., *Hind Swaraj or Indian Home Rule*. http://www.mkgandhi.org/swarajya/coverpage.htm

Landow, George P. "The 1857 Indian Mutiny (also known as the Sepoy Rebellion, the Great Mutiny, and the Revolt of 1857)." *Victorian Web*. http://www.victorianweb.org/history/empire/1857.html.

"London Vegetarian Society 1888–1969." *International Vegetarian Union*. http://www.ivu.org/hisory/vfu/lva.html.

Mahatma Gandhi Research and Media Service. http://www.gandhiserve.org/

"Noncooperation: Prelude to Home Rule Movement." *Indiansaga*. http://www.indiansaga.info/history/non_cooperation.html.

"Partition of Bengal, 1905." *Banglapedia*, http://banglapedia.search.com.bd/HT/P_0100.HTM.

Ruskin, John. "Unto This Last." *Electronic Text Center, University of Virginia*. http://etext.lib.virginia.edu/etcbin/toccer-new2?id = RusLast.xml&images = images/modeng&data = /texts/english/modeng/parsed&tag = public&part = 1&division = div1

South African War Virtual Library. http://web.archive.org/web/20021001085917/www.bowlerhat.com.au/sawvl/

INDEX

Abdulla, Dada, 37, 43
Ali Brothers, 124, 132
Amritsar, 127, 129–30
Anasuyabhen, Shrimati, 122
Asiatic Registration Amendment Ordinance, 89–91, 93–94, 96–97, 100, 104–5

Besant, Annie, 25, 68–69, 124, 130–31
Bhagavadgita, 24, 25, 75
Black Act, 89–91, 93–94, 96–97, 100, 104–5
Boer War, 65–66, 84, 91, 93
Botha, Louis, 91, 93, 103, 104
British Raj, 3, 125

Caste system, 3–4, 7, 30, 67
Chamberlain, Joseph, 60, 72–74
Champaran, 119
Churchill, Winston, 145, 152, 154
Colonial-Born Indian Educational Association, 49
Congressional Working Committee, 143, 145–46, 149, 153–54

Dada Abdullah & Company, 37, 46–47, 58–61
Desai, Mahadev, 101, 153
Dyer, Reginald, 127, 128

East India Trading Company, 34

Gandhi, Chaganlal, 73, 78
Gandhi, Devadas, 62–63
Gandhi, Devdas, 141
Gandhi, Harilal, 31, 73, 78, 84, 101; birth of, 17; difficulty with father, 61; marriage of, 84
Gandhi, Karamchand (Kaba), 1, 3, 7, 12, 15–17; accident, 8; death of, 12; early life of, 1–2; illness, 10
Gandhi, Karsandas, 1, 7
Gandhi, Kasturba, 12, 18, 77–78, 115; background, 5, 6; on

Brachmacharya, 150; death of, 153; dress, 57; illness, 87–88; marriage of, 6–8; as mother, 36, 72–73; pregnancy of, 16–17, 33, 63; reading, 5–6, 8–9, 31; in South Africa, 57, 61–62, 79, 82, 106; as wife, 9–10, 31, 48, 52, 55, 66, 85

Gandhi, Laxmidas, 1, 6, 16–20, 30–33; as head of family, 16, 34, 83–84

Gandhi, Maganlal, 73, 89, 117

Gandhi, Manilal, 36, 71–73, 142

Gandhi, Mohandas K., 1, 4, 5, 12–17, 19–27; and abolition of indentured servitude, 119; attacked over TARA, 94–96; as barrister, 31–33, 36, 45, 48, 50, 75–77, 101; and Boer War, 66; boyhood, 2–3, 11–12; and celibacy, 63, 85; at Champaran, 119–20; and Christianity, 45; and Congress, 54, 67–68; death of, 156; denial of worldly goods, 83; discrimination toward in South Africa, 38–42; Durban riot, 58–60; in England, 20–26; fasting, 147, 156; as father, 48, 61, 78; film biography of, 156; "The Green Pamphlet," 52; and *hartal*, 126; and health issues, 125, 138, 149, 150; and Hitler, 151; as husband, 9, 10, 48, 62; and indigo strike, 120–22; and Khalifat Conference, 130; at Kheda, 122–23; and Kumbha fair, 118; as leader in South Africa, 46–51, 73–76, 89–97, 99–112; and Lord Irwin, 138, 143–45; marriage of, 6–8; and medicine, 33, 87; meeting with Smuts, 93–94; and Muhammad Ali Jinnah, 139, 150, 152; nursing others, 54, 71–72, 78, 87–88; as outcaste, 18, 30; and Phoenix Settlement, 81–82; and plague, 53, 78–80; president of Home Rule League, 131; and Round Table Conference, 142–46; and Salt March, 140–41; Simla Conference, 154; and Simon Commission, 137; and spinning, 134; spirituality of, 46, 75; and Theosophy, 25; vegetarianism, 21, 23–24, 32, 71–72, 80–81, 110; and women, 131; as writer, 52–53, 91, 103; War conference, 124; World War I ambulance corps, 116; Zulu War, 83, 84

Gandhi, Nandkunwarba, 16, 17

Gandhi, Putliba, 2, 11, 16–17, 18, 29–30

Gandhi, Raliatben, 1, 18, 54

Gandhi, Ramdas, 62, 78, 141

Gandhi, Tulsidas, 12, 17, 33

Gita. See *Bhagavadgita*

Gokhale, Gopalkrishna, 55, 68, 71, 77, 100, 112, 115; death of, 118–19; in South Africa, 104, 105

Government of India Act of 1919, 129, 132

"Green Pamphlet, The," 52, 58, 60

Harijans, 147, 148, 155

Harijan, The, 147, 148, 151

Harischandra, 5

Immigration Restriction Act, 101
Indian Independence Act of 1947, 155
Indian National Congress, 55, 66–67, 90, 129; Annie Besant as president of, 124; annual meeting of, 132; discusses India as independent nation, 103; Muhammed Ali as president of, 134; and Rountable Conference, 142, 143, 146
Indian Opinion, The, 77, 80–82, 89, 95, 97, 103, 106, 111, 128
Inns of Court, 22
Irwin, Lord Edward Frederick Wood, 137–38, 142–46

Jallianwalla Bagh massacre, 128
Jinnah, Muhammad Ali, 130, 131, 138–40, 148–52, 154–55
Joshi, Mavji Dave, 16, 17

Kallenbach, Hermann, 104, 115
Kashmir, 155
Kathiawar peninsula, 1, 15
Khadi, 133, 134, 142
Khalifat conference, 130, 133
Kheda, 121–24

Lely, Frederick, 17
London Matriculation, 23
Lord Ripon, 48, 49

MacDonald, Ramsay, 139, 146, 147
Mazmudar, Tryambakrai, 19, 20, 23, 24
Mehta, Pherozeshah, 29, 35, 53–54, 67, 118, 120, 147; and Congress, 54, 67; meets Gandhi, 20–21
Mehtab, Sheikh, 10, 11
Mirabehn, 137, 147, 150, 153
Modh Bania caste, 4, 7, 18
Montagu-Chelmsford Act, 129
Muslim League, 103, 124, 149, 150, 152, 154

Naidoo, P.K., 109
Natal Indian Congress, 49, 51, 59, 73, 101
Nehru, Jaharwalal, 129, 138–40, 144–46, 148–56
Nehru, Motilal, 129, 134, 139, 143
Newcastle, 106, 107, 108

Orange Free State, 44, 46, 64, 110

Phoenix Settlement, 82, 84–85, 97, 106–8, 117
Pioneer, The, 51–53
Polak, Henry, 80, 82, 84, 110
Purna Swaraj Day, 140

Queen Victoria's Diamond Jubilee, 53

Round Table Conference, 142–46
Rowlatt Act, 126, 129
Ruskin, John, 80, 81
Rustomji, Parsi, 59, 60, 81, 96–97, 101

Sabarmati Ashram, 126
Salt's Plea for Vegetarianism, 21
Samaldas College, 16
Satyagraha Ashram, 118, 121, 128
Satyagraha Sabha, 126
Shravana Pitribhakti Nataka, 5

Simon Commission, 137, 139
Singh, Bhagat, 145
Slade, Madeleine, 137, 147, 150, 153
Smuts, Jan Christian, 93–95, 97, 99, 100, 103–5, 109, 111–12
Swadeshi, 103
Swaraj, 103, 118, 127, 131, 143
Swarajya Sabha, 131

Theosophical Society, 25
Theosophy, 25, 75
Tilak, Bal Gangadhar, 54, 123, 129–31, 132
Tolstoy Farm, 104, 106, 109
Treaty of Sevres, 131

Unto This Last, 80, 127

Wacha, Dinshaw, 53, 67
West, Albert, 21, 64, 80, 81, 111

Young India, 128, 138, 140

Zulus, 37, 64, 83
Zulu War, 83, 84

About the Author

PATRICIA CRONIN MARCELLO has penned nine books, including Greenwood Biographies of the Dalai Lama, Gloria Steinem, and Ralph Nader, and written for national magazines.

JAICO PUBLISHING HOUSE

Elevate Your Life. Transform Your World.

ESTABLISHED IN 1946, Jaico Publishing House is home to world-transforming authors such as Sri Sri Paramahansa Yogananda, Osho, the Dalai Lama, Sri Sri Ravi Shankar, Sadhguru, Robin Sharma, Deepak Chopra, Jack Canfield, Eknath Easwaran, Devdutt Pattanaik, Khushwant Singh, John Maxwell, Brian Tracy, and Stephen Hawking.

Our late founder Mr. Jaman Shah first established Jaico as a book distribution company. Sensing that independence was around the corner, he aptly named his company Jaico ('Jai' means victory in Hindi). In order to service the significant demand for affordable books in a developing nation, Mr. Shah initiated Jaico's own publications. Jaico was India's first publisher of paperback books in the English language.

While self-help, religion and philosophy, mind/body/spirit, and business titles form the cornerstone of our non-fiction list, we publish an exciting range of travel, current affairs, biography, and popular science books as well. Our renewed focus on popular fiction is evident in our new titles by a host of fresh young talent from India and abroad. Jaico's recently established translations division translates selected English content into nine regional languages.

Jaico distributes its own titles. With its headquarters in Mumbai, Jaico has branches in Ahmedabad, Bangalore, Chennai, Delhi, Hyderabad, and Kolkata.

SINCE 1946